FATHER~~LESS~~ *more*

Becoming the man *God* intended me to be

FATHER~~LESS~~ *more*

Becoming the man *God* intended me to be

JAMES POLNICK

FATHERMORE, Polnick, James

1st ed.

Subtitle: Becoming the Man God Intended Me to Be

Unless otherwise indicated, all Scripture quotations are taken from the Holy Bible, New Living Translation, copyright © 1996, 2004, 2015 by Tyndale House Foundation. Used by permission of Tyndale House Publishers, Carol Stream, Illinois 60188, USA. All rights reserved.

Scriptures marked KJV are taken from the KING JAMES VERSION (KJV): KING JAMES VERSION, public domain.

Scriptures marked NIV are taken from the NEW INTERNATIONAL VERSION (NIV): Scripture taken from THE HOLY BIBLE, NEW INTERNATIONAL VERSION ®. Copyright© 1973, 1978, 1984, 2011 by Biblica, Inc.™. Used by permission of Zondervan.

Scriptures marked ESV are taken from the THE HOLY BIBLE, ENGLISH STANDARD VERSION (ESV): Scriptures taken from THE HOLY BIBLE, ENGLISH STANDARD VERSION ® Copyright© 2001 by Crossway, a publishing ministry of Good News Publishers. Used by permission.

Scriptures marked NRSV are taken from the New Revised Standard Version Bible: Anglicized Edition, (NRSVA) Copyright© 1989, 1995, Division of Christian Education of the National Council of the Churches of Christ in the United States of America. Used by permission. All rights reserved.

Scriptures marked NASB are taken from the NEW AMERICAN STANDARD BIBLE (NASB): Scripture taken from the NEW AMERICAN STANDARD BIBLE®, copyright© 1960, 1962, 1963, 1968, 1971, 1972, 1973, 1975, 1977, 1995 by The Lockman Foundation. Used by permission.

This book and its contents are wholly the creation and intellectual property of James Polnick.

This book may not be reproduced in whole or in part, by electronic process or any other means, without written permission of the author.

ISBN: 978-1-957173-39-9
Copyright © 2023 by James Polnick
All Rights Reserved

DEDICATION

This book is dedicated in memory of my mother **Barbara Ann Paxton** who loved me unconditionally and whose constant involvement in my life made it a little easier for me to grasp the Heavenly Father's love for me. I love you, Mom, and cherish your memory!

I dedicate this book to my wife **Gina** who is my best friend and love of my life and to the ones who made me a father: **Ashlyn, Sterling, Jayden** and **Brighten**. Being your dad is my greatest joy and I am so blessed that God chose me to be your dad. I also wish to include in the dedication of this book my additional children, **Emily** and **Ezekiel**, who are married to my two oldest children and also my first-born granddaughter **Evangeline** who captured my heart upon her arrival. You all are my greatest treasure!

This is also dedicated to **all the men** God placed in my life to teach me His ways. Although I have mentioned several who influenced me greatly in this book, there are many more. God knows and I hope you know. Thank you for pointing me to Jesus!

FOREWORD

It's an honor to be given the opportunity to write this foreword for my dad. I've known this man my entire life, and now in my late twenties I can say what a joy it is to grow up with a father who has now become a friend.

My dad has always had a larger-than-life personality and it's been a rarity to not have my dad's reputation precede me. His reputation has opened doors for me and my siblings that I know we have failed to acknowledge numerous times. As a child I thought my dad was perfect, and he could do anything and everything. Whether it's writing a Christmas production, being a florist, photographer, or a pastor, my dad had no limits in my eyes. Now as an adult, my perfect ideology of my dad has changed and morphed into a new awareness of the grace of God in my father's life. In this book, you will hear from a man who had every opportunity to give up and to walk away from his healing. By no means is my dad a perfect man, but he is a liberated man. I hope that as you read this book you are awakened to the Lord's overwhelming pursuit of your heart. My dad, like many of us, had a void in his life that no earthly man could fill. Yet, through the grace and obedience of many Godly men, my dad was able to find his Heavenly Father and his inner healing. I pray that as you read this book you are reminded that our God takes our brokenness and redeems it for His glory. My dad would not be the man of integrity and faithful Christ-follower that he is if it were not for the men you will read about. I am forever grateful for the obedience of the godly men who invested into my dad to break generational curses that I am now a product of.

My dad has done and continues to do the hard work to live in healing. My dad is not a perfect father, but he was sure to introduce me and my siblings to the perfect Father. I hope that this book is another resource for you to meet Him as well.

Ashlyn Polnick-Lee

TABLE OF CONTENTS

	INTRODUCTION	i
1.	CONFUSED & CRUSHED	1
2.	GOOD THINGS & GOD THINGS	19
3.	HONOR & HONESTY	37
4.	FAITH & FEAR	55
5.	FAMILY & FOOTPRINTS	75
6.	LOVE & LOOT	91
7.	DISCIPLINE & DISCIPLESHIP	113
8.	CONSISTENCY & COMPASSION	131
9.	DEDICATION & DEVOTION	145
10.	COURAGE & CONFIRMATION	161
11.	PURSUIT & PERSEVERANCE	173
12.	MESSY & MIRACULOUS	187
13.	MY TWO GREATEST TEACHERS	201

INTRODUCTION

Within the heart of every human is the desire to be loved and to love in return. God made us that way because He is love. When we find Him, we find unconditional love, but we do not always trust His love like we should. We are born into a very flawed world full of imperfect people, into imperfect families, as imperfect people. Our search for love and acceptance begins upon arrival. It is a parent's job to provide nurture and reveal to their children the love and acceptance they need. There is even a greater responsibility on the father to do this because his child's (or children's) ability to find God's unconditional love and trust depends on it. When the "earthly father" connection is not right, it makes it hard for the Heavenly Father connection to be right. It makes it difficult for a child to understand God as Father and for His sacrificial love to be found.

The role of a father in the life of a child is so vital. There are character qualities that must taught and caught that only a father can provide. When a father is missing, there is a great void. Statistics for decades have revealed the problems associated with the father being absent from the home and not present in the lives of his children. A recent statistic revealed that seven million American fathers were absent from the lives of their minor children.

Boys without a dad present in their lives struggle with their identity and development as men, and they live daily with feelings of rejection. Many lack purpose and find it hard to be productive as they live with the rejection associated with the knowledge that their father chose to turn his back on them or take no interest in them.

Many girls become sexually active and have even become pregnant at a young age when their fathers are absent, abusive or fail to show them the love and attention they need. Without a father's affirmation to develop their worth and identity, daughters grow up with low self-esteem and feel a lack of worth. Many fatherless sons are filled with anger, and many fatherless daughters are left emotionally crippled. When the love of a father is missing, it causes his children to search for love in wrong places.

There are alarming statistics about the fatherless. Children from fatherless homes account for 63 percent of youth suicides, 71 percent of teenage pregnancies, 90 percent of the homeless population, 85 percent of those with behavioral disorders, 80 percent of rapists, 75 percent of those in substance abuse centers, and 85 percent of youth in prison. Children without a father involved in their lives are more likely to fail in school and be forced to repeat a grade and are twice as likely to be hyperactive, have conduct issues and social and emotional problems.

Fatherlessness is a serious problem. I am not just talking about men who choose to abandon their families, but I am talking about absent fathers who are too busy with work, who are unable to fulfill their responsibilities by loving, caring, protecting and teaching their children right from wrong. I am talking about men who choose to prioritize other things above God, their wife and their children.

The spiritual void of this fatherless generation is greater than the physical and emotional. Heaven and hell are real places, and that makes finding the Heavenly Father a more urgent issue. When the earthly father connection is not right, it makes it difficult for children to connect with God as their loving Heavenly Father.

It is hard for a child to trust in a Heavenly Father when they can't trust their earthly father. Comfort, rest and security in another person can only be found if there is trust. Trust must be present to have a healthy relationship with anyone. A father who cannot be trusted paints a picture that can cause the child to feel like Father God shouldn't be trusted.

It is not by coincidence that God chose to identify with us as family. He chose the word father. We all know what a father is and what he is supposed to do. Even if we did not have an earthly father who was constant in our lives or who treated us well, we understand what a good father should look like. God placed that idea in our hearts from the beginning and all of us have that need within us to be valued, cherished, protected and loved. That is what our earthly fathers are supposed to provide for us, but that does not always happen in life. For various reasons, children are left empty and fatherless. God promises that when earthly fathers fail, He will step in and become the Father that we need. Psalm 68:5 describes Him as: *"A father to the fatherless. A defender of widows, is God in his holy dwelling."*

In Luke 11:2, Jesus taught us to address God as Father. *"Jesus said, 'This is how you should pray: Father, may your name be kept holy. May your Kingdom come soon.'"*

God's love for us is described in several verses in the Bible like that of a loving parent:

"Then you will ask in my name. I'm not saying I will ask the Father on your behalf, for the Father himself loves you dearly because you love me and believe that I came from God" (John 16:26-27).

"Never! Can a mother forget her nursing child? Can she feel no love for the child she has borne? But even if that were possible, I would not forget you" (Isaiah 49:15).

"And I will be your Father, and you will be my sons and daughters, says the LORD Almighty" (2 Corinthians 6:18).

God chose a masculine form, that of a Father to us, to show us His strength, protection and provision. Throughout scripture God repeatedly promises to take care and provide for widows, orphans and the fatherless.

"Though my father and mother forsake me, the Lord will receive me" (Psalm 27:10).

God knew in advance that there would be earthly fathers who would fail in their responsibilities. He offers a solution to help us find the love, acceptance, protection and provision we need. He steps up and steps in and fills the role of a Father Himself.

"However, those the Father has given me will come to me, and I will never reject them" (John 6:37).

God desires to become the Father that we need, and He uses other men to replace the father void in our lives and show us His ways. A fatherless boy looks to anyone who will be proud of him, love him and accept him. A young man needs validation and needs to be taught and learn various lessons to succeed in life. If he can find a healthy, Godly example to look at in another man as a mentor or coach, then his life can be impacted with God's truth. Most importantly, the character of God can be seen in their examples, and the young man can find direction to help him develop a relationship with the Lord so he can succeed and flourish in the absence of an earthly father.

That fatherless boy was me.

That is what this book is about. It is my spiritual journey and how God became a Father to me and taught me how to be a man and father through the lives of the many men He placed in my path. Those men impacted my life and have helped me become the son, husband, father and pastor I am today. By watching their examples and how they lived out their faith, I learned many things that I needed to know in life. Most importantly, I learned about the unconditional love and acceptance of God that I so desperately wanted and needed.

Many of these men did not or do not even realize the impact they had on my life. I want to point out that none of these men were or are perfect. They all had or have flaws, but God has a track record of using flawed people to accomplish His purposes in life. I also know this to be true because God has used me with many flaws to make a difference in the lives of others. A life surrendered to Him is something He can always use.

My heart behind writing this book is first and foremost to honor God as my Heavenly Father. He has taught me so much, and all the glory belongs to Him! He is truly a good, good Father.

My prayer is that if you grew up lacking the attention you needed from your earthly father or he was missing or absent for whatever reason, that you will come to know the unconditional love of the Heavenly Father and experience a relationship with Him in a very real and tangible way. His presence is real. My hope is also that in your void of a father, by faith you will give your hurt, heartache and emptiness to God and let Him become the Father you need.

I pray that you will look around you, like I did, and be able to identify the men He has placed in your path to help you learn from to become the man or the woman that God designed you to be. I also hope that this book will encourage men to reach out as mentors and take time to be God's hand extended to the fatherless generation who so desperately hunger for "dad" and who need the direction of a Godly man in their lives. May this book serve as a reminder that others are watching you, and your life impacts those around you for good or bad without even you knowing it.

> **And you saw how the LORD your God cared for you all along the way as you traveled through the wilderness, just as a father cares for his child. Now he has brought you to this place.**
>
> *Deuteronomy 1:31*

── Chapter 1 ──

Confused & Crushed

*The LORD is close to the brokenhearted;
he rescues those whose spirits are crushed.*

Psalm 34:18

WHEN I THINK back to my childhood, for as long as I can remember I felt like I never fit in. Something was off. There was a feeling of rejection that seemed to follow me around.

My mom was my constant, and one thing I never doubted was her love for me. She was overprotective, and I had a bond with her greater than anyone else. I used to think that my problems and my confusion might stem from having an overprotective mother, and that may be part of the reason, but I recently found out there was another reason why she was so overprotective of me. I will share that reason in a later chapter. I just knew that something was off as a child, and I did not know what it was.

Although I had a father, I remember from an early age that my mom would never let him correct me. They eventually divorced, and because of the lack of a male figure in authority over me, I was a sissy and a momma's boy. I did not mind it when I was little, but as I grew older it caused me heartache. I was made fun of in school and by kids in our neighborhood. I just never fit in. I was blessed to have a sister who was two years older than me who loved me dearly and looked out for me. Until I learned to defend myself, she was quick to rise to my defense if someone picked on me. She is still that way and I am blessed to have her in my world and on my side.

My parents divorced when I was in kindergarten. I remember how heartbroken my sister was when my parents separated. She cried often, and I never really understood her hurt. I remember feeling something wasn't right, and I felt bad that dad wouldn't be living in the house with us anymore, but I also felt that my mom was all I needed, and I would be alright.

> I was too young to realize the void my dad's absence in my life would leave.

Now I realize how unhealthy my new situation was. Every child needs their mother and father to teach them different things. It is part of their development to help them grow into balanced, mature adults. That was missing for me. I was too young to realize the void my dad's absence in my life would leave. If a father is absent as children are growing up, they tend to view God as distant and uncaring. That was how I felt.

My mom remarried when I was in first grade. My stepdad was seven years younger than her and never really became a dad to me. I felt that we were always in competition with one another for my mother's love and attention. My mom always told me that he was jealous of our relationship. So, from the get-go, things were way out of balance. There seemed to be no standard of right and wrong in our home. The rules changed as each situation defined how they chose to view things in the moment. It was hard to know what was acceptable or unacceptable because there was never a consistent standard. It changed from situation to situation. This caused a lot of confusion, especially for a child. I am thankful they provided for me and my sister materially when we were growing up, but we needed spiritual direction more than anything. They could not give us that because they did not serve the Lord. I am thankful that after I was grown, my mom found Jesus and served Him until her passing.

> Looking back, I know God was always there and He was always working.

It is truly by the grace of God that I'm who I am and where I am today. Early on, my mom told me that from the time I was born, she felt God had something special for me. Looking back, I know God was always there and He was always working. I know He had a plan and that is why things turned out as they did, even though I went through a lot of hurt and pain. I always clung to my mom's words about me, and then one day when I became older, I found this truth in God's Word:

> *"For I know the plans I have for you," says the LORD. "They are plans for good and not for disaster, to give you a future and a hope."*
>
> Jeremiah 29:11

This wasn't just my mom but a word directly from God. As I said, my mom did not always live for the Lord, but she knew of the Lord, and in those years, God placed people of faith around her to direct her toward Jesus. My grandparents on my mom's side were both alcoholics, so my mom went through a lot to get where she ended up and get me where I am today.

I honor her for that.

THROUGHOUT my mom's life, seeds of faith were planted that would eventually grow and bring forth a harvest. Her employer at a truck line where she worked, Jean Rose, became her dearest friend and had the greatest impact on her life in so many ways, especially her spiritual life.

Jean was a beautiful lady and woman of God and a great example to my mom. My mom wanted to be like her and cherished Jean's memory until her own death. I take comfort in knowing that they are together in heaven today. I loved and adored Jean also and considered her a classy lady and someone who loved Jesus. I am so thankful for the impact she had on my mother and me.

God also used the PTL Club with Jim and Tammy Bakker to influence my mom spiritually. I remember every morning waking up for school and sitting on the floor in her room in front of the TV watching PTL while she fixed her hair, listening and believing every word with childlike faith. I am certain that many seeds were planted in me, many I am unaware of today, from those many hours of watching Jim and Tammy preach and sing.

I truly cannot write words to adequately describe my love for my mom. Imperfect, yes, but still my mom and my constant, and I cherish her deeply.

MY DAD remarried a few years after he and my mom divorced. I have some fond memories that I will share in another chapter about what I learned from him.

From the beginning, there was a disconnect with my dad and I never knew why. My dad favored my sister, and my mom favored me, and it was obvious to anyone who knew our family. We grew up thinking it was no big deal. It was just the way it was, and I felt it was normal. As I grew older, I realized just how out of balance it was and how it caused a deficiency in our lives.

> My dad became a friend to me, a distant friend.

My dad became a friend to me, a distant friend. A father cannot just be a friend to his children. He needs to be their constant support, an advisor, someone who trains them how to get through the tough things in life by being a living example of how to succeed. I needed that. I may not have known it then, but I know now that I missed out. I believe he did the best he could to be a father considering the circumstances he faced, and I harbor no hard feelings. I just had a lot to learn in life and about life, and he was not there when I could have used his example on how to become a man.

MY MOM and my dad both had a very strong work ethic and provided for us the best that they could. That meant they worked a lot, and we were frequently left to fend for ourselves. I think that is all they knew to do. I learned that things don't just happen, you must work at it, and that money does not grow on trees. We never went without food or material needs, but we did miss out on making memories and spending quality time together. More notably, they left our spiritual growth up to the Christian school that we attended.

A Christian parent's primary responsibility is to reveal God to their children by teaching them about Him and His ways through day-to-day interactions in life. My parents could not teach us something they did not have themselves. Although my dad attended church from time to time and took us, he knew God in a religious way and did not have a personal relationship with Him.

Parents who know Jesus are called to teach them God's ways and help them to find an eternal purpose for their lives. To do this, parents must be intentional and led by the Holy Spirit.

Direct your children onto the right path, and when they are older, they will not leave it.

Proverbs 22:6

The example set before me at home did not have any spiritual value. I do not blame my parents for this. I blame it on the enemy and the sinful world we are born into. At a young age, the home I was brought up in was just all I knew, and I told myself that life was this way. I found out different later. After I found the Lord, I soon realized that I had learned more what not to do and how not to live from my family than how to live right. The Lord was not a priority in my parents' homes as they grew up, so He did not become a priority in our home either. We were a "Christer" family. In other words, we only went to church on Christmas and Easter.

THERE IS one period of time in my childhood that is very cloudy. I don't remember a lot of good that happened during that time because of the impact of the bad that overshadowed it. They say that when a child goes through something traumatic, sometimes they block out things mentally. I can only guess that this might be the case for me during these dark years. After my mom's recent death, some of these feelings came to the surface for me.

> I needed my dad's guidance in dealing with this rather than carrying this secret with me for so many years.

During this dark time, from the age of about eight until I was twelve, I was exposed and introduced to pornography in my home. Back in the day, it was not as accessible as it is today and was in magazine and video form. Needless to say, once it gets hold of you, it is hard to stop the lust in your imagination from taking root. It did, and I struggled with it until my mid-twenties when the Lord delivered me and set me free. When He set me free, I was free indeed! I know a lot of men who have told me that they have struggled with this for decades, but that is not my story. I am thankful to God that He swiftly intervened and divinely took the desire away.

It was during those early years that I was sexually abused, leaving me confused and crushed. I carried guilt and pain from this for many years and felt shame for what happened. I always thought it was my fault. I was made to believe that, until I became old enough to realize that I was a child and that my predators were adults.

I wish I could have told my mom or my dad, but the disconnect did not allow it. I needed my dad's guidance in dealing with this rather than carrying this secret with me for so many years. I could have healed more quickly.

I never told my mother because I knew it would break her heart. I also knew she might take the law into her own hands, and someone could end up dead. I did not want any hatred and unforgiveness toward anyone to keep my mom from finding Jesus and making heaven her home.

> If God truly loved me and was always with me, then why would He allow horrible things to happen to me?

The closest I got to revealing what had happened in those dark days was telling my close friends that I would reveal something after my mother died but not before, because it would be too much for her. I am thankful God gave me a friend years ago who went through the same thing when he was a child. I was finally able to share this with him and find a little healing.

AT AN EARLY age I learned about God, but I did not really know God. He was a God at a distance somewhere far away to be held in high esteem, but not a God who truly loved me and who wanted to be a Father and friend to me. I eventually went through confirmation class in the eighth grade and was confirmed into the Lutheran Church. Something was still missing in my search to know the Lord deeply, and I could not put my finger on it.

As I entered high school, my mom put me in an evangelical Christian school. It was there that I was introduced to what it meant to have a relationship with Christ. While there, I heard teachers and preachers talk about the love of God, something hard for me to fathom. If God truly loved me and was always with me, then why would He allow horrible things to happen to me? It brought a lot of confusion and questions that I needed answers to. I thought that if He knew all things and knew about the abuse, then He was not much of a loving God.

> Deep within me, I wanted to believe,
> and I wanted to give God a chance.

There was so much that I didn't understand. I wanted to believe what I was being told about God, but it seemed as though the life that I felt Christ offered me was far from any life I had witnessed being lived out in my family. That even if God did forgive, He would not be interested in forgiving me. There was no way I was worth it.

Even in my confusion, God placed people in my path who told me truth and consistently preached and showed me God's love. Deep within me, I wanted to believe, and I wanted to give God a chance. The hurt I lived with was real, and I knew I was broken and needed to be mended. I did not like myself or my life and felt I had nothing to lose by repenting and asking Jesus to come into my life.

> I knew I needed to change and hoped
> that maybe God could really help.

People around me who knew me back then never realized the dark place I lived in. I was the fun guy, the life of the party, and I disguised all my pain with humor. I knew I needed to change and hoped that maybe God could really help. On a Wednesday in a chapel service back in 1982 at the Christian school I attended, when the principal Stephen Collins gave an altar call, I gave my heart to the Lord for the very first time. It was the first time, because I fell away many times after that, but the Holy Spirit was always working. I think I got saved every week for a while after that, because I would get convicted of my sins and need to repent.

I learned later that is the Holy Spirit's job, and that He is the One who drew me to a saving knowledge of who Jesus was and is today.

> **And when he (the Holy Spirit) comes, he will convict the world of its sin, and of God's righteousness, and of the coming judgment.**
>
> *John 16:8*

When we are convicted by the Holy Spirit, we must decide how we will respond. I responded with surrender. I knew I was broken and needed help and healing. I had a crushed spirit and had nothing to lose by giving God a chance.

I had felt Him drawing me to Himself before, but I had not fully trusted Him and in fact had ignored Him. I know now to be careful not to quench the Spirit of God that is kindled in us at salvation but to nurture it daily through the Word of God and not ignore His promptings.

> Some fathers may sincerely care about their children but be unable to translate that care into an authentic expression of love.

It was a long road for me. I did not have an earthly father who could connect me to the Heavenly Father, one who could provide an example to follow or spiritual guidance to receive, or at least I thought that. I was so distant from my earthly father, felt so disconnected and empty, that it was hard for me to comprehend that God the Father and His "love" would be any different. It is hard to believe by faith in a "God the Father" that you can't see, when the father that you can see is not really interested in you, and you don't feel loved by him or that you are a priority to him. This is not a jab at my dad. It was just the way it was, and I felt this way for numerous reasons.

AS I GREW older, the Holy Spirit taught me that I can't expect someone to love me unconditionally like God does if they don't have Jesus in their life. This freed me and brought healing to feelings I harbored toward my parents when I realized this truth. They needed Jesus, and at that point in my life, them finding Him became my mission.

In the world today, we are surrounded by countless examples of fathers who contradict what God intended a father to be. Some fathers may sincerely care about their children but be unable to translate that care into an authentic expression of love that will resonate in the heart of their child (or children). I think that was the case in my circumstance.

Perhaps it has to do with the way love is expressed to them by their parents. My dad never really told me, "I love you," and when I would say, "I love you," he would reply, "Me, too." It always bothered me when I was a teenager, but as I grew older, I remember I never heard my grandparents tell him "I love you" either. They never said it, just showed it.

> God is love, and you can't give away
> what you don't have.

I needed to be told. I have since learned that my love language is words of affirmation, so speaking "I love you" is what I needed because that speaks love to me. I also learned that you can't expect someone to love you unconditionally like God does if they don't have Jesus in their life. God is love, and you can't give away what you don't have.

MY JOURNEY in the Lord has been a long process. I was

confused, crushed and broken, and the road to healing was long. I hated myself at times, especially when I would fall back into sinful patterns again and again. I did not understand grace and felt that every time I failed, I was doomed for hell.

But God never gave up on me even when I gave up on myself. I wish I knew then what I know now as I daily stand on this passage in Lamentations 3:22-23. It will forever be a favorite of mine:

The steadfast love of the LORD never ceases; his mercies never come to an end; they are new every morning; great is your faithfulness.

Lamentations 3:22-23

The Holy Spirit came into my life at salvation, and from that moment on, I had Him. The bigger impact is that once I welcomed the Holy Spirit to fill my life, He had me. There is a difference.

When I let the Holy Spirit have me, He was able to work in me and allow His purpose and plans for my life to unfold. I had a lot of baggage, a lot of hurt, habits and heartaches to overcome. There was so much about God the Father I did not know. There was so much about being a man of God I did not know. I only knew what my mom had taught me, and she was not a man. I had an absent father who did not have a relationship with the Lord but only knew Him in a religious way.

As the Holy Spirit began to work, I attended church and Bible class, and things started to change. I began to realize that God had placed the right people in my path who were around me to teach me how to be the man of

God that He wanted me to become. Everything about my earthly father connection that I had missed, He was going to show me Himself. I could depend on Him to teach and train me through other men along my journey.

> Just as God has a plan for our lives and wants to write our story, so does the devil.

And that is what He did. God revealed His Word to me, and I watched it play out in front of me in the flesh.

I wanted to know Him. I wanted to trust Him. I wanted to live right and for Him. I wanted to be whole. I wanted to go to heaven when I died. I wanted a Father to love me and let me know it!

As I grew in wisdom in the Lord, I began to understand His Word and how things work in the spiritual realm. Just as God has a plan for our lives and wants to write our story, so does the devil.

For God is not the author of confusion but of peace, as in all the churches of the saints.

1 Corinthians 14:33 (KJV)

So if God does not bring confusion into our lives, we can assume the enemy is responsible. The evil one wants to change up the story of our lives any chance he can get.

I have had to remind myself of this throughout the years. If I find myself confused, God is not in it. He operates with peace. I tell myself this when I am faced with difficult decisions I must make.

I am a different man today because of God's grace and mercy, because I have allowed the Holy Spirit to work in me. I have been delivered from the crushing pain and addiction that confusion from the enemy brought into my life. I forgave my abusers, and the Lord showed me that they too had suffered abuse of some sort, and that they carried hurts, also. They needed Him, too. I began to pray for them to find Jesus and find healing.

> God does have a plan and a story to write in your life.

I wondered if I could ever be a husband and father after all this brokenness. I am so blessed that God healed me and allowed that to happen. I married the most beautiful girl inside and out on May 21, 1994. Gina and I have four wonderful God-dedicated and God-loving children: twins Ashlyn and Sterling, Jayden and Brighten, all of whom have a heart for Him. I am also blessed to claim two additional children: a daughter-in-love, Emily, and a son-in-love, Zeke, who are married to the twins. I recently became a grandfather of a beautiful baby girl, Evangeline Jona. My life is full. I am so blessed to know God, serve Him and experience His work in my daily life. The family He gave me is my greatest treasure.

My mom and dad are both in heaven today, and for that I rejoice. God revealed Himself to them individually, and they both surrendered. My dad was a tough one. In sickness he broke. I witnessed my mom in the last couple of years in her life make a major shift from focusing on the things in this world to things that matter in the next. I am heartbroken from her passing, but I am full of hope. One day I will see them again, and our home and relationships in heaven will be perfect.

God does have a plan and a story to write in your life. His story is full of twists, turns and adventure. He will work out even the bad seasons for good and for His glory. He will place people along our paths to fill any void that we lack and teach us His ways and all that we need to know. Everyone who truly desires to serve and obey the Lord will be directed by the Holy Spirit as they seek to find and fulfill His purpose.

> God began to be a Father to me and placed men in my life to love me and show me His ways. When He did, I realized that my scars may be deep, but God's love for me is deeper!

I had a father-void and was spiritually fatherless, but after I surrendered my life to the Lord and let the Holy Spirit work in me, I began to see that God had placed all the right people—men and women—in my path to teach me how to be the man of God that He wanted me to become and to reveal His truth to me. God began to be a Father to me and placed men in my life to love me and show me His ways. When He did, I realized that my scars may be deep, but God's love for me is deeper!

You may feel as though you are fatherless, but you don't have any excuse to stay that way. God promises us that He will be a Father to the fatherless and reveal His love to us. He will heal our brokenness and write His story through our stories, if we seek Him and allow the Holy Spirit to work in us.

> *Let us fix our eyes on Jesus, the author and perfecter of our faith, who for the joy set before him endured the cross, scorning its shame, and sat down at the right hand of the throne of God. Consider him who endured such opposition from sinful men, so that you will not grow weary and lose heart.*
>
> *Hebrews 12:2-3 (NIV)*

Chapter 2

Good Things & God Things

And now, dear brothers and sisters, one final thing. Fix your thoughts on what is true, and honorable, and right, and pure, and lovely, and admirable. Think about things that are excellent and worthy of praise.

Philippians 4:8

I DO MY best to practice and live by the words in this verse. The enemy does his best to attack us in our minds, because he knows that if he can get us to think like he does, in a negative way, he can get us to believe it in our hearts.

What we believe in our minds gets in our hearts, and we begin to live it out and react to it. The mind is the starting point for behavior. The evil one speaks lies and condemnation until he gets the emotional response that he is looking for. It no longer matters what I felt as a child;

neither does it matter what my earthly father did or did not do; it only matters that I am able to comprehend in my mind what my Heavenly Father says about me and believe in His love for me. Once I learned this life-changing truth from God's Word, things changed.

Finally, I began to live in victory.

THE BATTLE in the mind is a continual battle, and we must choose to defeat the enemy in our mind with our sword – the Word of God. The more I stay consistent in reading the scripture, the more I defeat the enemy, something I must do daily. The devil may tell me one thing, but I tell him what God says, and I think good things. Thinking on good things and Godly things is a choice, and although it may be a continual battle at times, it is worth the fight. Learning this truth set me on the path of healing.

> I could not see how God could get any glory if my story threw others under the bus and drew attention to the hurt and pain I went through.

For many years I felt like I was supposed to write a book about my life's journey, not to draw attention to me, but to share what God has done for me and in me. I wanted to tell others where He brought me from; that He can do the same for them; and that He heals and can bring peace into the dark places of their lives as well.

I wanted and still want to draw attention to Him.

A couple years back I decided it was best not to share my story, because I could not see how God could get any glory if my story threw others under the bus and drew attention to the hurt and pain I went through. After a personal and shocking revelation about my own life in January of 2021 and my mother's death in September 2021, God and I had a serious talk. The decision to write this book was settled. I felt God impress upon me to write about good things and what He has done, and if I made that my focus, He would get the glory.

This is what I set out to do, because it is my heart's desire is to point others to Jesus and please Him above all others.

IN PHILIPPIANS 4:8, Paul draws a conclusion that he shares with the church at Philippi and, through our study of the Bible, with us. Paul wants the church (and that includes us) to grow and become mature disciples who in return can create other healthy disciples.

> Paul recognized the power of our thoughts ... that the way we think determines how we feel and how we live.

We see throughout scripture the pattern of discipleship as one person and one generation stay committed to the Lord and teach others of God's love and reveal the resurrection story to them. Paul knew this would not be possible if we could not think correctly. Paul recognized the power of our thoughts. He understood that the way we think determines how we feel and how we live. The word *think* means to ponder, to give proper value to, and to allow the thoughts you think to influence the way you live.

Paul says in this passage to first think on what is true. God is Truth. His Word is Truth. So, if we look at God, who He is and what the Bible says, we will discover this Truth.

Truth and trust are what our
relationships with others are built upon.

Whatever is true is also respectable. This means truth should be respected because it comes from the only One we can hold high with upmost respect for His character, wisdom and position as Creator of all. Our reverence and worship are due to God who is Truth and who displays His Truth to us clearly in His Word.

The Bible is a teacher of truth. When we embrace truth and think on those things that are true, we are choosing to think on God things. When we live truth, we are living from a place of respect. Truth requires respect, even if we don't always see it in the messed-up world we live in. God respects and rewards truth. Truth and trust are what our relationships with others are built upon.

If a father (or any parent) has a problem lying either to or in front of his children, it can cause great damage to their character development and produce destructive results. Children learn more by what they see and hear than what they are just told is truth. I learned this the hard way more than once with my children, even when what I said was intended as a joke.

The day after a presidential election, my wife Gina and my youngest son, 5-year-old Jayden, were at the store checking out when Jayden called out, "Dad said we aren't having Christmas this year."

"Why?" My wife was puzzled.

"Dad said that if such-and-such became President, we were not going to have Christmas."

Things we say in humor can be taken literally by our children, sometimes to our great embarrassment. That day, my wife was mortified. The lady checking them out had voted for the newly elected president. We laughed about it for years afterwards, but the bottom line is that our children need to be able to trust what we say. I called it joking, but it was a lie to Jayden.

> Children form what is true based on the example set before them, whether the example is a reality or a lie.

Both Jayden and I learned something that day, me as a parent and Jayden as a child. I learned to be careful what I say, and if I do say something in jest that he might overhear, to clarify exactly what I mean. Jayden learned that I like to pick at him; not everything I said was always true; and that I like to get him rattled up.

CHILDREN FORM what is true based on the example set before them, whether the example is a truth or a lie. One of the obstacles I had to overcome early on in my life was not to lie. I eventually learned I could get a lot further in life by telling the truth than trying to manipulate my way through life by telling lies, but growing up, I was flooded with mixed signals, and it was sometimes hard to distinguish the truth. I ultimately came to an awareness that at times truth hurts, but it can ultimately be healing. Most importantly I came to understand who the father of lies is. Read with me:

> *For you are the children of your father the devil, and you love to do the evil things he does. He was a murderer from the beginning. He has always hated the truth, because there is no truth in him. When he lies, it is consistent with his character; for he is a liar and the father of lies.*
>
> John 8:44

Just as we have a Heavenly Father in God who loves us deeply, we must also realize that there is a counterfeit father of lies who wants nothing more than to destroy us. The Word says that liars in the end get to swim in a lake of fire and burn forever. As a child, I could only compare that to the worst sunburn I had ever had, where I could not sleep or get comfortable because the pain was constant and almost unbearable. We must look to God, for God is Truth, His Word is Truth, and the scripture says to find what is true.

Paul also says to think on those things that are **honorable**, **right** and **pure**. When we think on those things that are **honorable**, we are thinking on those things that bring worth and honor in the world, into a situation, into our lives and into the lives of others. I have chosen to think honorably by honoring the men who have impacted my life in this book.

When we think honorably, it simply means that we love what is right and choose to do what is right because it is right. To do right, one must think about what is right. We will always choose to act based on our perception of what we think is right.

Many people see what is right and wrong differently. Some feel that what is right for you might be wrong for them, and what is wrong for them may be right for you. Right is right and wrong is wrong, and there should be no confusion. Our standard of defining what is right must be based on the Word of God. What the Bible says goes. We either believe that or we don't. We either embrace its truth or ignore it. Paul challenges us to let our thoughts be honorable and right, and when they are, they will also be pure.

The word pure here means holy. This is talking about moral purity and holy living. We will live out the way we think, so we should strive to have holy thoughts. It's all in the noggin, as my dad called it.

> Whatever we put into our minds is what is going to affect the way we live our lives.

Thinking on pure things means that we fill our minds with thoughts that are virtuous, clean, Godly and not according to evil influence or the standards of this world. We let the scripture and what it says guide our thoughts. Whatever we put into our minds is what is going to affect the way we live our lives. Scripture must be the standard that we live by.

Pure thinking should fill every area of our lives: the places we go; the things we watch; the activities we engage in and all that we do. All our thoughts should be morally clean to be characterized as pure. When we make the choice to think about pure things, it will lead us away from sin and closer to God.

JESUS SAID it's not what's on the outside that makes us impure but what's on the inside that comes out of our hearts.

> ***It's not what goes into your body that defiles you; you are defiled by what comes from your heart.***
>
> *Mark 7:15*

This is why it is so important that we take seriously hiding God's Word in our hearts because it is the only thing that will keep our lives pure. David reflected on this in the following passage:

> ***How can a young person stay pure? By obeying your word. I have tried hard to find you— don't let me wander from your commands. I have hidden your word in my heart, that I might not sin against you.***
>
> *Psalm 119:9-11*

I pray that you see the importance of living your life daily in His Word. Many of the addictive behaviors I overcame in my life I attribute to time well spent in God's Word. I learned to effectively think on pure things, and to do that, I had to follow the advice that Paul gave the church at Corinth:

> *We destroy every proud obstacle that keeps people from knowing God. We capture their rebellious thoughts and teach them to obey Christ.*

> 2 Corinthians 10:5

One translation says that we "take captive every thought to make it obedient to Christ." We do that by seizing and throwing off all thoughts that are contrary to what God's Word says. Paul the great apostle tells us in his letter to the church at Ephesus:

> *Throw off your old sinful nature and your former way of life, which is corrupted by lust and deception. Instead, let the Spirit renew your thoughts and attitudes.*

> Ephesians 4:22-23

We need the Holy Spirit in our lives and working in us. We need to allow Him to renew our thoughts and attitudes so that they will remain pure and holy. We need the Holy Spirit to work in us to convict and renew our thoughts and attitudes in order to live pure and holy. It is important that we take our thoughts captive because our thoughts control our lives. They can also decide our destiny.

Let me remind you that Jesus is coming back for a pure and spotless bride. We are His bride. We don't have to be perfect because He is, but we need to be pure and have our sins covered by His atoning blood. I am thankful that when we fail, His grace is sufficient and that He sees our hearts. Keep your heart pure and keep your life's lamp full of the oil of the Holy Spirit because Jesus is coming much sooner rather than later.

LASTLY PAUL says to think on those things that are **admirable**. Another word for admirable is good. We are called to think on good things and on good reports.

We admire people and things. We admire heroes, athletes, actors, leaders, pastors and even family members. We admire the beauty of God's creation, and we admire the knowledge and creativity we see in other people. We admire the accomplishments in others that we see.

It appears to some that Paul is reminding them to look at objects of wonder and be in awe about things they see around them. That is not what I think Paul has in mind or the message he wants to convey. He is trying to convey admiration and its meaning as a feeling of wonder, pleasure or approval. Instead of objects, Paul says we should be looking with wonder and admiration and be in awe of a person – God Himself who is the only one who is good. Jesus tells us this in scripture:

> ***"Why do you call me good?" Jesus asked him. "Only God is truly good."***
>
> Luke 18:19

All these good things are God things because they are works He accomplishes in and through people. God is good and the things we admire in others and in the world are the work of His hands. The only good part in us is the good that God does through us, the good things that He has placed there. Paul's hope is that God be admired because of the good that He does through us, so that He will get all the glory.

One translation of this passage says to think on those things that are commendable. That means anything that is of a good report and speaks highly of others. Thinking this way helps you to let go of the negative things that others have done and celebrate the positive. None of us is good. All of us need God's grace and forgiveness. It is a choice to think on good things and God things. A good first step along this path is to avoid taking offense (or becoming negative) and ask God to let us see others through His eyes of love.

> God can do a much better job of fixing things in the spiritual realm than we can in the natural.

I believe it is a waste of time and energy to think on anything but good. We can pray about the bad going on in the world and the people we know who have done bad things and give it to God. Don't allow evil things to consume your thoughts.

I must also say be careful and watch what you say about others. Just because a person fails badly in life does not mean you have to repeat to someone what they did. This is gossip. Don't gossip, whether you believe it's true or not. It is our job to pray for others and about the problem and situation. God can do a much better job of fixing things in the spiritual realm than we can in the natural. We are to think good of people. Even the worst person you know has something good and admirable about them.

This applies to yourself also. Thinking good thoughts is healing. If you tell yourself over and over how bad you hurt, how awful you were treated, how someone abandoned you and how horrible you were treated, you are never going to get better. In fact, the opposite will happen. You will become bitter. Sharing things like that will only breed destruction. Your children are watching, others are watching, but most of all, Jesus is watching.

I choose to think on commendable, admirable things and live free.

I COULD write this book and tell you over and over how all the men in my life have failed me to some degree and rip them up for it. In the chapters ahead I could tell you all the bad things I know about them and how I learned what not to do from them, but instead I want to share good things and God things so that God can get the glory and I can honor the men God placed in my life who led me to know Him greater.

> Paul says our thoughts should be directed towards that which is admirable, and not that which is offensive.

As we meet other people, we have a choice of how we perceive them. We can focus on their good qualities or the bad things we notice in them. Paul says our thoughts should be directed towards that which is admirable, and not that which is offensive. Our perception should lead us to uncover the God things in other people, even when all we can see at first seems bad.

As I was writing this, I was sitting in a local food establishment, and the men at the table sitting next to me had smut mouths (every other word this one guy said was the "f" word). I still chose to greet them with a smile, and we made small talk. I found kindness in them, and I chose to see them as God sees them – in need of His love. They simply needed Jesus to do a work in their mouths.

Kindness is part of the fruit of the Spirit. I saw a little hint of kindness in them, which meant He was working in them. I could have ignored them and asked to be moved to another table to keep from typing the "f" word into my manuscript, but instead I chose to see them as men that God loves and desires to do a work in. I stayed and continued to converse some with them hoping that perhaps they might see the goodness of God in me.

> Choose to focus on the good and Godly things you see in others.

Think on good things today. Avoid the offensive. Focus on the admirable. Choose to focus on the good and Godly things you see in others. If you do, you will see God working, and the work He does is always excellent and praiseworthy.

As a father I believe it is important that I keep my heart pure and that I live a holy life as an example before my kids so they can see God's goodness revealed in me and come to admire Him as their Heavenly Father. I believe the way we choose to live will reflect the way our children choose to live.

PAUL ENDS this passage by telling us to think on things that are **excellent** and **praiseworthy**. To think on excellent and praiseworthy things, we must think about God's goodness and His work in our circumstances, our lives and the lives of other people. The good He does in our lives far outweighs any of the bad things we have to endure.

> God places great responsibility on men
> when He calls them to be the spiritual
> leaders of their homes.

Be careful not to allow the enemy to place the bad things around you in a magnifying glass. There may be five things wrong, but there are a hundred things right. With God in our lives, the positive will always outnumber the negative if we choose to see things through His eyes instead of the devil's lens. I speak from experience. I almost quit the ministry and thwarted God's plan for my life and for my family by focusing solely on the bad things going on. I am thankful the Holy Spirit got my attention and I saw the excellent and praiseworthy things happening and decided to celebrate and think on those things.

God places great responsibility on men when He calls them to be the spiritual leaders of their homes. That responsibility should not be taken lightly as the faith of our families depends on it. Husbands and fathers are called to serve their families and imitate Christ. We should be devoted to our family's needs spiritually and help them grow in their relationship with God. Our attitudes, the way we think and the way we choose to see things, are so important for spiritual development and growth in our families. Our families will only know Jesus as much as we know Jesus.

I encourage all parents to teach their families that spiritual warfare is real.

We must heed Paul's message and fix our thoughts on what is true. We must speak and live the reality of the Word. We must take the apostle's advice and think on what is honorable and right, on what is pure. We should do all we can to live holy and acceptable lives for the Lord and be an example for our families to follow.

Paul says to think on good things that are excellent and praiseworthy. Don't borrow the enemy's magnifying glass to look at the negative things in life, because God's goodness always far outweighs the bad things. Count your blessings and you will find there are many more of them.

FATHERS SHOULD provide encouragement, guidance, grace, support and protection for their families. I encourage all parents to teach their families that spiritual warfare is real. The devil is real and wants to destroy what he can touch. Love your children in the good times and the bad times so they can see God's love. To the men reading this, our wives and children need to know that we are willing to lay down our lives for them just as Jesus laid down His life for us.

> ***Fathers, do not provoke your children to anger by the way you treat them. Rather, bring them up with the discipline and instruction that comes from the Lord.***
>
> *Ephesians 6:4*

I pray that God will let me see things through His eyes and that I will always choose to see good things and God things in life. As I pray that for myself, I pray that for every person who ever reads these words. I also pray that fathers will step up and realize that they matter and walk into their God-given roles as the spiritual leaders in their homes.

In upcoming chapters, I will share the good things and God things that I have learned from watching and following the example of many men (fathers) that God placed in my life to fill the void left unmet by my earthly father.

> Even the bad things educate us in a good way, if we allow God to reveal truth to us in that situation.

The greatest void was of a spiritual nature, but there were also many life lessons I missed out on learning because of his absence. I want to remind you that none of the men I write about were perfect. All my experiences with them were not good, and from some I learned what not to do. I learned from their mistakes, and I found that even pain can be a teacher.

Every lesson we learn in life does not come from good things. Even the bad things educate us in a good way if we allow God to reveal His legitimacy to us in that situation. Each of these men impacted my life in a real way, and I saw Jesus working through them to reveal Himself to me and to teach me the ways of the Heavenly Father.

My prayer for you as a reader is that God will use what I learned from them to encourage and teach you also.

Chapter 3

Honor & Honesty

Rubin Polnick

I MADE the choice to focus on good things and God things and to count my blessings despite relational differences with my dad.

While my relationship with him was lacking in many ways, I learned two things from him by watching his life, and they have helped shape my own character.

My dad lived out Honor and Honesty.

RUBIN POLNICK was the only dad I knew and had in my life from the very beginning. He was the first and only man I ever called Dad. He was present when he could be, and for that I am thankful.

There is a difference between being physically present and actively present in a person's life. My dad was sometimes the first, but equally often, he missed the mark with the second. I don't blame him for his absence, although there were times I felt he could have made a greater effort. Divorce with visits every other weekend has a way of creating a relational distance.

He was a great man who grew up in a family with six other siblings. He became a machinist and worked for his father. When his dad retired, he took over the business until he was forced to retire himself for health reasons. I have several fond memories of being at the shop with him and for a short time working there cleaning valves and brushing off heads. It was hard work, but I learned it was ok to get dirty sometimes.

> My sister and I have many childhood memories with our dad from the time our parents divorced until our early teens.

Some of my favorite memories as a child were with him. We traveled to Giddings, Texas, and went fishing, hunting and bowling, and we played bingo and made many memories with my grandparents, aunt and uncle and my cousins. My dad liked sports also and played softball for several years on various leagues with a couple of his brothers. I remember going to his house on the weekends and going to watch him play on Friday nights. He was active when he was younger, and I did most of my outdoor activity with him while in grade school.

He was also part of a bowling league, and for a summer I followed in his steps and joined a bowling league. My sister and I have many childhood memories with our dad from the time our parents divorced until our early teens. I remember him taking time out for us and even attending our school athletic games; and on the weekends he would take me and my friends to do fun things. All my friends loved him, and those I am still in contact with today talk about all the fun we had with my dad.

MY RELATIONSHIP with my dad was up and down depending on what was going on in his life. If I needed anything of monetary value, he would do his best to provide it. While in high school, every Friday I would stop by his shop, and he always had twenty dollars to give me for the weekend. I learned pretty quickly that one perk from coming from a divorced home was that I could ask my mom and dad for the same twenty dollars every weekend and be the richest kid in the school from Friday to Monday.

> I knew that real love could only be found
> in a relationship with Jesus Christ.

A downside was that my dad was always looking for love. And because of that, he was married three more times after my mom. He grew up in the Lutheran Church and knew of God but did not have a personal relationship with the Lord. I always prayed He would find love. I knew that real love could only be found in a relationship with Jesus Christ, and after I experienced salvation in Christ, my prayer for him was that he would find Jesus in a very real and intimate way.

I am thankful that eventually he did. Through his illness his heart softened, and he became sensitive to the things of God before he died. My prayers were answered, and I know one day that I will see him again in heaven.

On my last visit with him a couple of days before his passing, I told him I loved him and it was ok to go if the angels came to take him. I told him that I knew our relationship was lacking in this world, but that when we both got to heaven one day, things would be different and all would be good. I remember that day him telling me clearly and verbally what I had needed to hear him say all my life: "I love you, too." I know he is now experiencing real love like never before in heaven. I honor him as I write this because that is what he taught me to do.

Honor everyone. Love the brotherhood. Fear God. Honor the emperor.

1 Peter 2:17 (NRSV)

MY DAD was a man who honored others. He honored his parents, veterans, law enforcement, civil servants and those in authority over him. I can recall as a child when we met those in the service or law enforcement that he would acknowledge them and thank them for their service. He also taught us to always respond to adults with, "Yes, ma'am," and, "Yes, sir," and, "No, ma'am," and, "No, sir." If an adult entered the room, we were taught to stand and give them our seat to show them respect and honor.

Dad may not have agreed with everything those in authority over him stood for or did, but he showed respect to them because of the position they were in. His example, whether he truly knew it or not, was scriptural.

Pay to all what is owed to them: taxes to whom taxes are owed, revenue to whom revenue is

> **owed, respect to whom respect is owed, honor to whom honor is owed.**
>
> *Romans 13:7 (ESV)*

One of the most meaningful ways my dad showed honor was to his parents. The way he respected and honored his mother impacted how I honored and adored my mom as well. He always took time out to make trips to see his parents on a regular basis and when I was younger took me and my sister along with him.

My grandparents lived a couple hours away, and it was not out of the ordinary for him to close his shop on Tuesday afternoons about 4:30, throw us in the truck and drive to his mom's house to take her to play bingo at the local bingo hall. Later that night, we would drive back for work and school the next morning. Some of my sister's and my greatest memories were at that bingo hall. He lived out the first commandment with a promise well.

> **"Honor your father and mother." This is the first commandment with a promise: If you honor your father and mother, "things will go well for you, and you will have a long life on the earth."**
>
> *Ephesians 6:2-3*

This is something I tried my best to live by as well. I did well in honoring my mother but for various reasons was not always able to show my dad the honor he deserved because of the distance in our relationship. I was grateful to have the privilege to honor him and eulogize him at his funeral. I shared what a great man he was and how Jesus had come into his life and changed him for the better.

HONOR IS supremely important. It is part of God's value system that I think is overlooked in our world and lost in our culture. Honor positions us to receive all that God has for us in life.

According to the New Testament, honor means to hold at a great price, to esteem, to see worth in a person or things. It also means to recognize and show value to that which is dear to the heart. The opposite of honor is disgrace. More than anything, a person should be honored for their character rather than for than their achievements.

> **Fear of the LORD teaches wisdom; humility precedes honor.**
>
> Proverbs 15:33

Honor is always given to a person who is humble. It is not something a person can take. A person should never feel they deserve honor. Rather, it is something that they humbly receive for who they are and for what they do.

> **And no one takes the honor to himself, but receives it when he is called by God, even as Aaron was.**
>
> Hebrews 5:4 (NIV)

The Bible calls us to take honor seriously. Honor those in authority, including parents, bosses and government.

When we learn to do this, we will learn to honor God.

> **A son honors his father, and a servant his master.**
>
> Malachi 1:6 (ESV)

We are to honor those who serve, whether it is in the military, on the job, in the community or in the church. If someone serves you in any capacity, you should honor and respect them.

Those who minister to you should be honored in a special way. David in scripture was so attentive to this principle that he was careful not to do, say or even think anything that might dishonor God's anointed king, Saul.

> **The elders who direct the affairs of the church well are worthy of double honor, especially those whose work is preaching and teaching.**
>
> 1 Timothy 5:17 (NIV)

I have always taken this seriously. I never let a birthday, anniversary or celebration go by for the pastor I worked for over 16 years. I knew the weight he carried was heavy, and I looked for ways to serve him and make his load lighter. I have also been a part of celebrating the retirement and milestone birthdays of many ministers who have served the Lord faithfully who were worthy of honor.

SCRIPTURE SAYS we are to honor all people, including our spouses, children and friends. Those we are close to and love may seem easy to honor, but we are also called to honor those who are not so lovely, those who don't serve the Lord and even those we are not close to.

Be devoted to one another in brotherly love; give preference to one another in honor.

Romans 12:10 (NASB)

This verse takes honoring others to a higher level. It tells us that there is never an excuse to show dishonor to anyone. Perhaps the fact that we choose to honor someone that we don't even know well may cause them to see the love of God working through us. For the lost, the honor that we show them could lead to a revelation of God and their salvation.

It is easy to honor those who are deserving, but we honor God even more when we show honor to those who don't deserve it or that we don't even know. When we do this, we honor God, and above all else, the Bible tells us that we should honor God. We do this when we love Him and what is right; when we love truth; and when we love people, all people.

Now to the King eternal, immortal, invisible, the only God, be honor and glory forever and ever. Amen.

1 Timothy 1:17 (NIV)

We receive honor in return when we honor God and do what is right. Righteousness makes us honorable in the eyes of the Lord.

Whoever pursues righteousness and unfailing love will find life, righteousness, and honor.

Proverbs 21:21

God created us for honor. We are to give honor, and if we do, we will receive it. God wants to honor us.

HONORING GOD requires that we honor Him with our first fruits. The first of our wealth, week and weekday. I will share more about how I learned this the hard way in an upcoming chapter.

Sometimes in the middle of the storm it is hard to give thanks. Even if it is a sacrifice, do it anyway.

Honor follows easily out of gratitude. A thankful person will find it easy to show honor to God and others. Sometimes in the middle of the storm it is hard to give thanks. Even if it is a sacrifice, do it anyway. God's Word says to do so.

But giving thanks is a sacrifice that truly honors me. If you keep to my path, I will reveal to you the salvation of God.

Psalm 50:23

Be the kind of person that honors. It is a choice, but when we make the choice to show honor, we honor God.

> **The King will reply, "Truly I tell you, whatever you did for one of the least of these brothers and sisters of mine, you did for me."**
>
> Matthew 25:40 (NIV)

I am thankful that my dad surrendered his life to God and learned to honor the Lord before he left this world. He taught me about honor in other ways, but to see Him acknowledge God and honor Him before he passed away will be my greatest memory of him. He may not have done everything right when he was in the world (none of us can), but that does not matter now. What matters is that he learned this truth and honored the Lord. I believe that he received his reward in the end. I wonder what he thought when Jesus looked at him and said:

> **The master said, "Well done, my good and faithful servant. You have been faithful in handling this small amount, so now I will give you many more responsibilities. Let's celebrate together!"**
>
> Matthew 25:23

I admonish everyone reading this to create the culture of honor in your life.

MY DAD also taught me about honesty. He was an honest man who never made us promises that he would not keep. Because he was honest, if he said he would do something, he would.

He was a man of his word.

The LORD detests lying lips, but he delights in those who tell the truth.

Proverbs 12:22

As I reflect on my life, I truly never remember my dad telling a lie or asking me to tell a lie either. He desired to take the high road when it came to truth. I am thankful for his example. Being from a divorced home, I experienced a conflicted upbringing. I witnessed dishonesty in many areas of life while growing up, but I never saw any of that from my dad.

I lied about things that were not even important to get what I wanted.

Had I been around him more, perhaps my struggle with honesty while growing up would have been less. If I forgot my lunch at home and I called him, I knew he would show up with lunch at school. If I could convince him to say "yes" about something, he would make it happen. Sometimes I lied that I forgot my lunch just so he would bring me a hot lunch to school. I lied about things that were not even important to get what I wanted.

There were times I took advantage of him and lied to manipulate him. I was a pretty good actor and could be convincing over the phone. In college, I would call him and ask him to send me money through Western Union because I was sick and had to go to the doctor. This was when I was young in the faith and the Holy Spirit still had a lot of sanctifying work to do in me. I was wrong, and it was manipulative on my part. I've since repented, and I am thankful that the Lord freed me of this fruit of the devil — lying.

> Thinking back, I think I lied mostly because I wanted acceptance because I grew up feeling rejected.

Society does its best to play down lying, and to not make a big deal out of it. It's called a white lie, a half-truth, a fib, misleading information, exaggeration of truth and even stretching the truth, when it is just lying. I shared with you already that this was something I had a problem with when I was younger. I think I would lie to sound important or to cover something I had failed to remember that I had been asked to do. It was my way of not looking irresponsible or having to face the consequences for my actions. There were even times that I would begin a conversation with the intention of saying something that was true, but before I knew it, I found myself exaggerating and adding to the story. I think in general most people who lie do so because they feel telling the lie will give them an advantage in getting their way or possibly make them appear better than they are.

Thinking back, I think I lied mostly because I wanted acceptance because I grew up feeling rejected. I wanted to sound big! Regardless of the why, being dishonest is detrimental in the life of a person and causes their character and reputation to be tarnished and questioned. Once a person is known as a liar, it is hard for your opinion of them to change. I am thankful that with God all things are possible, and that He can make all things new. I am so thankful for the revelation I received about being honest when I found the Lord and that He set me free from the work that the father of lies, the devil, had planted in my character.

DISHONESTY CAN sometimes seem natural. People lie on their taxes, cheat on a test, lie about their age, even lie about complimenting someone about something they know is not true. I think keeping silent about something when you should have told the truth is also wrong as your silence supports dishonesty.

> Dishonesty costs a great deal in this world, but nothing compares to what it will cost in the next.

My dad set an example of honesty for me, and I am thankful for that, although it took many years for me to see it. Think how different our world would be if we all lived by the Ninth Commandment and never gave false witness against anyone and always told the truth. I bet courtrooms would be less crowded and cases would settle quickly. People would have a lot more money in their pockets because lying is very costly. Dishonesty costs a great deal in this world, but nothing compares to what it will cost in the next.

Jesus does not excuse our lack of truthfulness just because it is hard to be honest, or because we might get in trouble. He commands that we tell the truth. Honesty is not just words we speak, it is who we are. Jesus gives us truth that we need to remember and adhere to.

> **All you need to say is simply "Yes" or "No"; anything beyond this comes from the evil one.**
>
> Matthew 5:37 (NIV)

I love this verse. There is no need to craft a lengthy answer to persuade someone's thinking to be different in a situation when asked a question. The answer is either yes or no. The evil one, the devil who is the father of lies, loves gray areas because the truth is not in him. Don't be deceived by his ploy and fall into his trap.

Jesus, while speaking to His followers, left no gray areas when it comes to telling the truth. We are either children of God who are honest or children of the devil who are liars.

> **For you are the children of your father the devil, and you love to do the evil things he does. He was a murderer from the beginning. He has always hated the truth, because there is no truth in him. When he lies, it is consistent with his character; for he is a liar and the father of lies.**
>
> John 8:44

So when we lie, we are speaking the enemy's language and becoming like him. The devil knows the Word of God also, and he knows the consequences that will take place in the lives of people who are dishonest. He wants nothing more than for you and me to end up with him in the eternal lake of fire.

> **But the cowardly, the unbelieving, the vile, the murderers, the sexually immoral, those who practice magic arts, the idolaters and all liars— they will be consigned to the fiery lake of burning sulfur. This is the second death.**
>
> *Revelation 21:8 (NIV)*

WE LIVE in a day where we have more legal documents and contracts which mean less than at any other time in history. A person's word used to mean something. That's no longer the case.

I remember as a young child that my Pawpaw owned a Texaco service station, and he would do business on a handshake. People would come get gas when they needed it and then on payday come by and pay off their tab. A man's word meant something. In today's world we are forced to have contracts and legal documents for everything. Prenuptial agreements before marriage are the norm. It is no wonder that Jesus connects His teaching on divorce with His teaching on honesty. Marriage is the highest commitment that we make outside of our commitment to God. We need to let our "yes" be "yes" and let our "I do" mean "I do."

Being honest requires that we be transparent with others. This also requires humility. We do not have to pretend to be someone we are not. We cannot be honest if we are living behind a false front and not letting others see the real us, and we spend all our energy trying to uphold a lie trying to make others think that we are someone we are not. How tiring this must be to keep up with such a charade! Honesty means that we let people in on who we are, even if it means showing that we are less than perfect. We let them into our problems and even allow them to see that we are broken in places.

We must be real to heal. As Christ followers, we need to be real and authentic. We can't know everything or have all the answers, and we are not supposed to. We are all learning and a work in progress.

If we claim to have fellowship with Him and yet walk in the darkness, we lie and do not live out the truth. But if we walk in the light, as he is in the light, we have fellowship with one another, and the blood of Jesus, his Son, purifies us from all sin.

1 John 1:6-7 (NIV)

To walk in the light, we must be honest and transparent. No one is perfect, and we need one another to get through the struggles in life.

I think my dad stuck more to himself and struggled with a lot on his own. He lacked in the transparency part of life, I think, mainly because of his upbringing. I know I had a problem with it also. Once I completely surrendered my life to Christ, I found I was free to be me and I could be transparent with others. Some people liked me, and some didn't, and it is still that way today, but I am okay with it. God loves me! There is no use hiding anything, for in the end, everything will be revealed.

HONESTY AND INTEGRITY go hand in hand. Honesty is what you do, but integrity is who you are. Integrity comes from the word meaning entire or whole. It means that you are not going two ways at once. There are some people who live two different lives. I have heard about this more recently than ever before. It is heartbreaking to watch as the Holy Spirit exposes darkness in a person's life in an effort for repentance to occur. At the root of living like this is dishonesty and a lack of transparency. Somewhere along the way, people buy into the lie of the enemy and give in to his way of thinking. Then, their sin overtakes who they are. Sometimes they don't even know who they really are, creating a lack of integrity.

> Dishonesty is a cycle. One lie leads to another, and more lies have to be told to cover up the first lie.

We live in a world of denial. People expect to be lied to. Dishonesty is normal. But we do not belong to this world. We belong to a world where truth reigns – the Kingdom of God.

Being a Christian is not just following a set of beliefs or morals, it is a way of life. It is living in truth set free from a life of lies.

Dishonesty is a cycle. One lie leads to another, and more lies have to be told to cover up the first lie. Over time the person who tells the lie becomes unable to remember the truth anymore. When we find Jesus, we find truth.

Jesus answered, "I am the way and the truth and the life. No one comes to the Father except through me."

John 14:6 (NIV)

Jesus does not just speak the truth, He is the Truth. Our society says that truth is whatever you believe, but you can believe in something and be totally wrong. The Bible is our truth, and we need to live our lives in truth and honesty. Jesus is the Way, the Truth and the Life.

My dad, Rubin Polnick, was the first man to influence my life. I am thankful for his examples of honor and honesty. I know God used him to plant seeds of truth in me from a very young age, and I am thankful that they grew and brought forth fruit in my life. There were many more men that God placed in my path to show me His ways, and I am thankful for all the men God used to point me to the truth that is only found in Him and that would allow me to find a Heavenly Father in Him.

Chapter 4

Faith & Fear

Howard Burroughs

I WANT to start by saying that I will refer to Howard Burroughs throughout this chapter as **Brother B**.

In the era that Brother B came into my life, it was common within the church and church circles to call men and women Brother or Sister, signifying that you respected them as your brother or sister in Christ and as part of the family of God.

On the first day I arrived at the evangelical Christian school that my mom placed me in for high school, I sat next to a guy who would become my friend and that God would use to change my entire life. His name was Marty, and we hit it off as friends from day one. Brother B was his dad, and he was the Superintendent of the denomination of churches in the district in which the church school was located. He was stoic and his presence in any room was big, because he was someone special who was God loving and God fearing.

I was not raised nor had never been in a Pentecostal environment up to this point in my life. I knew the Lord in a religious way and had been through confirmation at the previous Christian school I attended, but the charismatic Pentecostal movement was completely new to me. I entered it blindly.

As you can imagine, I was a bit shocked.

> The very first weekend I went to Marty's house, I was introduced to his parents, Brother B and Margie.

I recall on my first day of school that we had chapel, and they were praying for someone to have his leg healed. I thought that everyone was crazy. I remember going home and telling my mom I did not want to go back to that school, and she convinced me to stay by saying that if I still felt that way come Friday, she would talk with my dad and see what they could do. I am glad God had it all planned out.

Marty and I quickly became great friends, and as the weekend approached, he asked if I wanted to come to his house for the weekend. I accepted his offer. By the time Friday came, I had forgotten about the crazy chapel service earlier in the week and was excited about all the new friends I had met. The very first weekend I went to Marty's house, I was introduced to his parents, Brother B and Margie. They were the most inviting and hospitable people I had ever met. They were kind and loving and seemed to take an interest in me and cared about me from day one.

I had never seen this type of interaction in a family, and it was something I admired from day one of being in their home.

On the first Sunday I was there, we all went to a large church across town, and Brother B preached. It was the first time I had ever heard Pentecostal preaching like that, and I listened intently as he shared the Word of God. He was amazing and had a gift of storytelling like no other preacher I knew. His delivery always pulled me in.

That first weekend was just the beginning of many weekends getting to travel with Marty, Brother B and Margie to many churches in the district as he preached. I took it all in and observed that the man I witnessed preaching God's love and grace and against sin in the pulpit lived it out in his daily life and in his home. I knew Brother B and his family had something different and special, and it was something I wanted to have – a living relationship with Jesus. His faith was real, and he lived what he believed.

> When the altar call was given, I could not wait to get to the altar and give all my mess to Jesus.

I found it in a chapel service at my school where I gave my heart to the Lord and began my journey of faith. It all started to make sense. The faith that Brother B preached and lived out before me meshed with the message that our school principal spoke about in chapel that day.

When the altar call was given, I could not wait to get to the altar and give all my mess to Jesus. There was still a lot I had to learn, a lot of baggage I needed to get rid of and a whole lot of sanctification work that the Holy Spirit had to do, but I gave in, and it began. It was the best decision I had ever made in my entire life. As I shared in a previous chapter, I fell away from the Lord many times after this, but the Holy Spirit always drew me back. I don't know what I would do without the Holy Spirit's work in my life.

> Brother B was the most like Jesus to me of any man on earth, and I looked up to him. He was real, and although not perfect, he was close in my eyes.

Brother B was the most like Jesus to me of any man on earth, and I looked up to him. He was real, and although not perfect, he was close in my eyes. He was perfect in the way he pointed people to Jesus, including me. I remember that he was excited to hear when I had given my life to the Lord.

I cannot write about him without writing about Margie. Margie played an important part in my faith journey and in who I became and who I am. She and I would stay up sometimes after Brother B and Marty would go to bed and talk. She taught me a lot about "doing the right things." She was born premature and it caused her to be hard of hearing, so she spoke loudly at times. I can still hear her voice in my head saying things to teach me like: *"Doing the right thing will not always make you popular with people, but being popular in God's eyes is what matters the most,"* and, *"Don't promote yourself. Work hard and serve and let God do the promoting."*

Little did she know that every time she spoke a truth like that to me, it was always what I needed to hear at just the right time. The Holy Spirit used her words to speak truth to me exactly when I needed it.

Margie loved me like a son, and every time I see her today, she reminds me of that. I cherish her and love her dearly as my spiritual mom. One of my greatest honors was that when I was ordained in ministry, Margie was my ordaining elder. To my knowledge, she was the first woman at that time to act as an elder. It was certainly fitting for me. I was also honored to be part of the last ordination class that Brother B graduated before he retired as Superintendent. Those are precious memories for me.

From Brother B, I learned many foundational things in my journey toward the Lord. What I recall most is that he lived out a genuine Faith and had a healthy Fear for the Lord.

> **Fight the good fight for the true faith. Hold tightly to the eternal life to which God has called you, which you have declared so well before many witnesses.**
>
> *1 Timothy 6:12*

Brother B taught me a lot about faith and the Christian pilgrimage. He was calm and I rarely ever saw him get really worked up or get upset about anything, I guess he knew it would do no good because the God he knew, served and preached about would work it all out and use whatever happened for his good.

And we know that God causes everything to work together for the good of those who love God and are called according to his purpose for them.

Romans 8:28

The only times I can remember him raising his voice was so Margie could hear him, likely because she didn't have her hearing aids in. He was calm and not easily shaken by things. I am certain it was because He knew where to channel the things that bothered him, to the feet of Jesus. He was a man of the Word and a man of prayer. It was just normal for him to have a Bible opened up near wherever he was seated at home.

I have tried my best to follow Brother B's
calm example through the years but
have not always been able to do it.

This calmness about him was peaceful, and if you were around him, the peace he felt could be sensed by you. He was hard to read at times, and it could be difficult to figure out what he was thinking, but you knew he was thinking; and you could trust that whatever it was, he and God were having a conversation about it in his head. I have tried my best to follow Brother B's calm example through the years but have not always been able to do it. God just gave him a double dose of peace and patience. I guess he knew he would need it having to deal with so many needy parishioners and problemed preachers.

PEACE IS PART of the fruit of the Spirit listed in the book of Galatians where we learn the character of God. When we come to know Christ and we welcome the work of the Holy Spirit in our lives and begin to grow in Christ, He develops this fruit in us. I saw this whole batch of fruit displayed in the lives of Brother B and Margie. I saw them in Marty also, but at this point in life, God still had a lot of work to do on Marty. He and I were typical teenage boys who were just learning what living a Christian life really meant.

> *But the fruit of the Spirit is love, joy, peace, forbearance, kindness, goodness, faithfulness, gentleness and self-control. Against such things there is no law.*
>
> Galatians 5:22-23 (NIV)

I witnessed love, joy, peace, patience, kindness, goodness, faithfulness, gentleness and self-control from watching their lives. Their lives showed me the whole faith package. For the first time this seemed real and attainable, and it was a life I wanted. I believed and I wanted to have equally great faith.

Faith is an active trust in God, a belief that what He says is true. Christians believe that Jesus came into the world and lived a perfect life, died on the cross on our behalf, and rose again victorious over sin and death from the grave. We trust in Jesus to save us from our sins. We have faith that He gives us His Holy Spirit as He promised and trust the Holy Spirit to do His work of sanctification in us. We live to honor God, relying on His forgiveness and trusting that His ways are best.

In addition, our faith results in action in our lives. For this to happen, we must believe in God and live for God.

Brother B preached his faith as truth and lived it each day. The same Holy Spirit that revealed this truth to him is the same Holy Spirit that revealed it to me.

Now faith is the assurance of things hoped for, the conviction of things not seen.

Hebrews 11:1 (ESV)

Faith is a result of teaching. Knowledge is important in faith, and we learn by what we are taught, what we read in the Word of God and by seeing others live out their faith in action.

Consequently, faith comes from hearing the message, and the message is heard through the word about Christ.

Romans 10:17 (NIV)

Our faith is established in what we hear and what we are taught from the Word of God. God uses people to teach us His truth. He used Brother B, Margie and even Marty to walk and live the gospel message before me when I was 13 years old, and for that I am thankful. By the unconditional love and patience they showed me, I saw faith in action. Their faith was alive.

> ***As the body without the spirit is dead, so faith without deeds is dead.***
>
> *James 2:26 (NIV)*

We are saved by faith, BUT good works should flow from that faith. We are not saved BY works but we are saved FOR works.

I AM THANKFUL and blessed that the works of faith flowed through the life of Brother B into my life. I also learned from him a healthy fear of the Lord.

> ***The fear of the L***ORD ***is the beginning of knowledge, but fools despise wisdom and instruction.***
>
> *Proverbs 1:7 (NIV)*

I didn't want to be a fool. I wanted to know all about Jesus! Most kids my age thought they knew everything, but I knew that when it came to the things of God how the Bible said to live, and that I was lacking and needed to learn.

By this time in my journey, I had heard many sermons by several different pastors and, honestly, I had established a fear of the Lord and lived a little in fear that if I did anything wrong that God was watching and waiting and ready to send me to hell.

Much of the preaching I was hearing, outside of Brother B's sermons, was mostly hell, fire and brimstone sermons and not many about grace. I remember having a hard time believing when God called me to the ministry, because I did not think I could stand up in front of people and yell and scream at them. That was what many preachers of that era did. I am thankful for them because they did scare the hell out of me many times, and I needed that, but I did not have a real knowledge of what it meant to have a fear of the Lord.

As born-again believers we should not
be living in fear of God's judgment.

Brother B and Margie lived in the fear of the Lord in a healthy way. As I began to understand what it meant to live in the fear of God, I looked at their lives, and their example brought balance and helped me figure it out.

As born-again believers we should not be living in fear of God's judgment, because we've had our sins atoned for by Christ. As followers of Jesus, we should not fear God's wrath, because Christ has taken upon Himself the punishment for our sins.

There is no fear in love, but perfect love casts out fear. For fear has to do with punishment, and whoever fears has not been perfected in love.

1 John 4:18 (ESV)

God is love, and so in Him there is no fear. The fear of God is not easily understood by those inside and outside of the church. The fear of the Lord is not a fear of being struck down by God when you sin and having a fear of hell hanging over your head, although that is a real fear for non-believers, but rather the fear of the Lord is a holy, reverent respect for God, for His Word and for obeying His commands. It is an awe kind of fear.

In the world we live in, as we see sin increase and evil increase, it is a direct result of a lack of fear of God. As this happens, people's hearts get hardened because they do not fear God and there is no limit to the evil things that can and will happen.

We pray, "Lord, heal our land," but there is no healing if there is no reverent fear of the Lord who is the only One who can heal. We cry out and declare *2 Chronicles 7:14* for help, but God tells us in in the first three words the problem:

If my people, who are called by my name, will humble themselves and pray and seek my face and turn from their wicked ways, then I will hear from heaven, and I will forgive their sin and will heal their land.

2 Chronicles 7:14 (NIV)

"If my people" are people who reverently fear Him. When we fear God, we walk humbly before Him, communicate with Him in prayer and seek His ways. We will obey what He says and keep our sin under the blood of Jesus.

Fearing God means having respect for Him and obeying Him. It means we acknowledge Him for who He is as Creator of all, Lord above all, and as being mighty and more powerful than anyone else. When we do this, we will act reverently toward Him and obey what He says. When we fear Him correctly, we will want to obey Him and do what pleases Him.

The fear of the Lord is connected to holiness and judgment. Fearing God means that you keep in line with His will, and in doing so, we are kept from living an on-going life of sin.

Because we have these promises, dear friends, let us cleanse ourselves from everything that can defile our body or spirit. And let us work toward complete holiness because we fear God.

2 Corinthians 7:1

Revelation 14:7 illustrates the fear of the Lord as it connects to judgment:

"Fear God," he shouted. "Give glory to him. For the time has come when he will sit as judge. Worship him who made the heavens, the earth, the sea, and all the springs of water."

Revelation 14:7

Why is fearing the Lord so important? Because fearing God is connected to judgment. If we don't fear Him, then He has the right to judge us. Many people in the world and even in the church are going to be shocked one day when they don't make heaven because they never learned to fear and love the Lord enough to obey Him. Do not resist

Him or ignore Him, but acknowledge Him as your Creator, Savior, and Lord and heed His voice and live according to His ways. Give your life to Him, live each day out of reverence to God and be saved from condemnation.

> **Therefore, there is now no condemnation for those who are in Christ Jesus, because through Christ Jesus the law of the Spirit who gives life has set you free from the law of sin and death.**
>
> Romans 8:1-2 (NIV)

Brother B lived in the fear of the Lord and was a great example to me as he lived what he preached. I saw a healthy fear for God play out in his life. I learned to stand in awe of God and that my obedience to Him should be driven out of respect, reverence and honor for who He is.

IT WAS DURING my teen years and in this time with the Burroughs family that I went to youth camp and felt the Lord call me to ministry. As I sat in my seat and the altar call was given for a ministry call, I felt the Lord say, "I'm talking to you." I did not fully know what that meant, but I know that what little faith I had in me said yes. I responded, yet there was still so much I did not know and needed to learn. The Lord reminded me of a passage I had heard before about Moses and feeling inadequate in what God had called him to do.

> **But Moses pleaded with the LORD, "O Lord, I'm not very good with words. I never have been, and I'm not now, even though you have**

spoken to me. I get tongue-tied, and my words get tangled." Then the Lord *asked Moses, "Who makes a person's mouth? Who decides whether people speak or do not speak, hear or do not hear, see or do not see? Is it not I, the* Lord*?"*

Exodus 4:10-11

I found rest in the fact that God equips those He calls and that with Him all things are possible. I did not know how this could happen, but I trusted that it would if it was truly God calling. Brother B and Margie were my greatest cheerleaders in my ministry calling. That is what made my pastoral ordination day extra special, the fact that they had played a part in my spiritual journey from the very beginning.

I hope to make an impact in the lives of others the way Brother B and Margie did in mine.

I have never forgotten where the Lord brought me from, and I hope and pray that Gina and I will be and have been a Howard and Margie Burroughs to someone else. I think of several we have invested in, but I hope to make an impact in the lives of others the way Brother B and Margie did in mine. The way they took interest in my life has shaped the man, father, and Christian leader I have become.

I have been truly blessed!

BROTHER B went home to be with the Lord in 2018 and received His reward. There is an old chorus song that he used to sing called *I Am Blessed*. Occasionally I think of it, and every time, I can hear Brother B's voice singing it in my head over and over.

That was his heart. I could write an entire book about Brother B and Margie, because they loved me big and impacted my life and many others in many ways. From noticing my shoes had holes in the bottom and slipping me a hundred dollars to buy a new pair to buying my wife and me new mattresses as a wedding gift so we would not have to sleep on a sunk-in mattress. They gave of themselves and loved us not expecting anything in return.

Brother B was quite the storyteller …
One special to me he would tell around Christmas.

Brother B was quite the storyteller, so I will end this chapter with one of his stories. He had a few that he considered to be fan favorites. One special to me he would tell around Christmas. It was about a group of children at a small neighborhood church. One day the children's church leader talked to the pastor about allowing the children to put on a Christmas Nativity on a Sunday morning. The pastor agreed but told her that they would need to practice. He expected there to be costumes, a set and that it all be done very well. The children's church leader asked the kids who wanted to be involved. Nine-year-old Tommy volunteered for the part of Joseph. His seven-year-old sister, Julie, would play the part of Mary. They had a baby doll for the part of baby Jesus.

The only open part left was the innkeeper. For this all-important role, she turned to an eight-year-old, red-headed, freckle-faced, bashful boy, and he reluctantly agreed. She instructed Joseph and Mary to borrow their parents' bathrobes and a pillow from the house to make Mary look pregnant. The director brought in a bathrobe for the little innkeeper. She gave them instructions as clearly as humanly possible when she directed Mary and Joseph to walk slowly down the center aisle, telling them how they would walk up the steps to the elaborate door on the stage labeled "Inn." She told Joseph that he was to knock on the door and say, "Please sir! Won't you let us in? My wife is great with child." That was it. The only line he was supposed to say. Just knock on the door and say only that line.

> The innkeeper's job was to open the door and simply say, "No room in the inn," the only line the innkeeper needed to say.

The innkeeper's job was to open the door and simply say, "No room in the inn," the only line the innkeeper needed to say. The little red-headed boy practiced it repeatedly. He would say the line and close the door. Once he closed the door, Mary and Joseph were to make their way to the side of the stage where the manger was waiting. In rehearsal, it was executed perfectly.

The Sunday morning arrived for them to act out the

Christmas story to the congregation. It was quite a large crowd that day, and the room was full of energy and excitement. At the right moment, the children's church leader directed Mary and Joseph to begin their journey down the aisle. Mary, with a big pillow under her mom's bathrobe, and Joseph in his dad's oversized bathrobe began their journey. As soon as the people noticed them making their way down the aisle, they burst into applause, cheering for Mary and Joseph as they made their way to the platform and the door of the "inn."

> Joseph, feeding off the energy in the room, decided he wouldn't take "no" for an answer and knocked on the door again.

It seemed that Joseph experienced something new that day. He had never been in front of a crowd until that morning and had no idea how much he would enjoy their applause. It was a high he had never known. Joseph knocked on the door of the inn, and the reluctant little eight-year-old innkeeper, with no previous acting experience, opened the door.

Joseph, boldly and with authority, delivered his line, "Please, sir! Won't you let us in? My wife is great with child." The crowd cheered! Joseph was overcome with satisfaction. The innkeeper responded exactly as he was asked to, "No room in the inn," and closed the door. Joseph, feeding off the energy in the room, decided he wouldn't take "no" for an answer and knocked on the door again.

The confused innkeeper again opened the door. "Sir, you just don't understand the desperate situation we are in. Look at her! You have to let us in!" The innkeeper, obviously shaken, squeaked out his line again, "No room in the inn." Joseph, not to be denied again, stuck his foot in the way of the cardboard door. "Sir, we could have this baby right here on the step of your inn. It would make a mess! Please give us a place to have this baby. This baby is going to be the Savior of the world! You just don't know it yet. Please sir, won't you make room in your inn?"

The little inn keeper, instead of reciting his line, gave in to the pressure of Joseph's Academy Award-winning performance, opened the door and said, "I know I'm not supposed to, but come on in!"

> I am so thankful that the Burroughs
> family made room for me in their home
> and hearts and let me "come on in."

Brother B would close the story by saying, "What that little innkeeper did that day is exactly what you and I need to do today. We need to say to the Lord, 'Come on in.'"

I am so thankful that the Burroughs family made room for me in their home and hearts and let me "come on in." My life took a different path because they did.

Howard and Margie were my second parents and my spiritual parents, and I will forever hold them dear to my heart. I thank all the Burroughs family and their extended families for welcoming me and always making a place at their table for me and my family.

My life forever changed the day Marty, Brother B and

Margie came into my life. I will share more about Marty later. He deserves a chapter all to himself.

> **The fear of the LORD is the beginning of wisdom, and knowledge of the Holy One is understanding.**
>
> Proverbs 9:10 (NIV)

Thank you, Brother B and Margie, for the knowledge of the Holy One that you instilled in me!

―― Chapter 5 ――

Family & Footprints

I have no greater joy than to hear that my children are walking in the truth.

3 John 1:4 (NIV)

Jack Dudley

ACCORDING TO the Barna Research Institute, one out of three marriages ends in divorce. It seems like marriages and families are falling apart all around us. Sadly, today the rate of divorce for born-again Christians is about the same as those who are not.

My parents divorced when I was 5 years old, so I never really lived in a home with two parents who stuck it out "for better or for worse." My parents were young when they married, did not know the Lord and fell into this divorce statistic. Marriages and families struggle in part because people do not understand the God-ordained roles of individual family members.

I was fortunate enough that shortly after I gave my life to the Lord, God began to place men in my path to teach me what Godly marriage and family looked like. One of those men was **Jack Dudley**.

WHILE ATTENDING a Christian youth camp in the Hill Country of Texas, I became friends with Jack's daughter, Kristi. Kristi had a best friend named Angie. Little did I know at the time how these two girls would impact my life for the better. They became like sisters to me and are still that way today.

After camp, we started hanging out together more often and that was when I was introduced to the Dudley family. Jack was surrounded by girls – his wife Peggy and his three daughters – and they are all beautiful inside and out. It did not take long with Jack for me to see what a marriage and family was supposed to look like.

Jack, Peggy and their daughters lived out Colossians 3:18-21.

> **Wives, submit to your husbands, as is fitting for those who belong to the Lord. Husbands, love your wives and never treat them harshly. Children, always obey your parents, for this pleases the Lord. Fathers, do not aggravate your children, or they will become discouraged.**
>
> *Colossians 3:18-21*

This passage in Colossians points out the Lord's design for family and the responsibility of different members within a family. God's idea of family wasn't something I understood, but Jack led his family to love and honor God and to love and honor one another. Respect resonated within the Dudley walls, and I wanted that.

> He had a joke with his daughters where he would tell them privately that each one of them was his favorite.

He had a joke with his daughters where he would tell them privately that each one of them was his favorite. The truth is they each were for different reasons, but he always wanted his girls to feel special.

Jack and Peggy loved and honored each other and set a great example of Love and Honor for everyone around them about what a Godly marriage should look like.

THE BIBLE tells us that wives are to submit to their husbands. Submitting to another person is an often misunderstood concept. It does not mean becoming a doormat. Peggy was never a doormat to Jack. She was adored and held in high esteem by him. I think people often get this "submit" to your husband thing wrong.

The man is not to be a superior ruler of the wife but an equal. As a pastor I often do weddings, and one of my favorite parts of the wedding dialogue says:

> "The woman in being created from man, or out of man, was not: out of his head to dominate, or to

be over him, nor out of his feet to be under him, or trampled upon by him, but out of his side to be equal with him, from under his arm to be protected by him, and near to his heart to be loved."

Marriage is about giving and taking. Marriage requires mutual sacrifice, honor, respect and the ability to forgive one another's faults.

People might think that because the wife is called to submit to her husband, she is less of a person or less important in God's eyes (and possibly in her own). This is far from the truth. I hear men quote *Ephesians 5:22* without looking at *verse 21* and *verses 23-25*. Here is what all these verses in Ephesians say together:

> **Submit to one another out of reverence for Christ. Wives, submit yourselves to your own husbands as you do to the Lord. For the husband is the head of the wife as Christ is the head of the church, his body, of which he is the Savior. Now as the church submits to Christ, so also wives should submit to their husbands in everything. Husbands, love your wives, just as Christ loved the church and gave himself up for her.**
>
> *Ephesians 5:21-25 (NIV)*

The couple is called to submit to one another to make their marriage work. The wife won't submit to her husband if she is not convinced that her husband loves her deeply, like Christ loves the church, and would be willing to lay down his life for her.

Jack loved Peggy like this. They submitted early in life to one another, just as they had submitted their lives first and foremost to Christ. Over a half-century of marriage is a testimony to this truth.

> Marriages create families, and families are dear to the heart of God.

Submission is voluntary on a couple's part. A wife must be willing to submit, and a husband can't force her to do it. When she knows in her heart that her husband is willing to give his life up for her, she submits to him as her protector. I have often told couples when I counsel them that for the wife to submit to the husband, she has to know that he would be willing to take a bullet for her. In premarital counseling, I tell couples that if they are selfish and not willing to sacrifice for one another, they should not get married. Marriage is a covenant and bond not to be entered into lightly and without great thought and prayer. Marriages create families, and families are dear to the heart of God.

Family is His design.

I have followed suit in my own life and tried my best to honor and love Gina in the same way Jack honored and loved Peggy. It has not always been easy. There are tough days in any relationship, but the couple who submits to God and one another will get the most out of their marriage. Marriage takes three – a man, a woman and God. This is God's design.

When a husband and father sets the spiritual path his family will follow, if his marriage is healthy, and the home is stable and grounded in God, the family will be healthy, and the chances are greater for the children in the home to follow the father's lead. I have known men who have been great spiritual examples for their children and things have still gone very wrong. Even when things do go wrong the children remember the example set before them and return and make things right.

In the book of Colossians, we learn the responsibility of children and how they are to respond to their parents in obedience, because when they do, it pleases the Lord.

> **Children, always obey your parents, for this pleases the Lord.**
>
> Colossians 3:20

Jack's daughters learned early in life that to please the Lord they needed to obey Him and be obedient to their parents. I witnessed a healthy, Godly fear of the Lord in his daughters and a great respect for Jack and Peggy from them. If the husband and the wife are fulfilling their roles, it will be easier for the children to obey because they find security in Mom and Dad's stable relationship. They also follow the example set before them and desire to have that kind of relationship themselves one day.

I also had the privilege of watching the way the entire family honored Peggy's mom and dad. (I lovingly called them Mamaw and Papaw.) This submission, honor and obedience thing was generational, and it was something that Jack and Peggy also did with their parents. I have also seen their daughters, their sons-in-law and grandchildren do the same to them. It is a beautiful thing to see a family love like this and pass it on from generation to generation.

THE LAST PART of the passage in Colossians 3:18-21 gives a message to fathers regarding their children. Paul tells fathers not to aggravate their children. He emphasizes that it will discourage them. As I look back over my childhood, many of the inconsistencies in my home certainly brought confusion and mixed signals, and it was aggravating at times.

Fathers, we must be fair when possible and not aggressive when correcting our children. We aren't to stir up or cause problems for them. There are several ways our children can be aggravated: through neglect, lack of love, being overly protective or critical, setting unrealistic goals for them, harsh discipline, showing favoritism or being critical of them. These can bring discouragement and create problems our children will be forced to deal with throughout their lives.

> Jack believed in me when others wouldn't or couldn't.

Fathers are not to be problem-makers but problem-solvers for their sons and daughters as they provide for them and live out an example before them. Jack was a great example for his family, his extended family and his friends; and he was always willing to help.

Jack believed in me when others wouldn't or couldn't. In my early twenties, I did not have a car or good credit, and he gave me $1,000 and put his credit on the line so that I could buy my first car on my own. This helped me to reestablish my credit and set me on a path to recovery.

Because he believed in me, I never wanted to let him down. I paid faithfully on that car until I was able to pay it off, before trading it in for a truck. Every time I made a payment, I pictured his face and felt so blessed that he was willing to take a chance on me. I felt that he was proud of me.

> I think that is what I needed most,
> someone to believe in me.

I am blessed to have had Jack and Peggy Dudley believe in me. I think that is what I needed most, someone to believe in me. If a husband and father wants to accept his place as the leader of the house, then he must also accept the responsibilities given to him by God. Children rely on their father to offer encouragement. When a dad fails to do this, it can have a long-lasting impact in a negative way on his children. If we want the blessing for our home that God wants to give to us, then we must also fulfill our responsibilities and lead our family to fear and love God.

Jack knew this and gladly served his family, loved and protected them and kept them in church. He was a great father and spiritual leader. He was generous, served on many civic boards, ministry boards, church boards and committees and had the heart of a servant.

THE LOVE a father has for his family is unconditional. When he loves them this way, they understand how the Heavenly Father can love them this way. Jack was good at this. His girls were not perfect, but his love for them was. I knew that they did not want to do anything that would displease their dad, and they felt the same way about their Heavenly Father.

> **So as to walk in a manner worthy of the Lord, fully pleasing to him, bearing fruit in every good work and increasing in the knowledge of God.**
>
> *Colossians 1:10 (ESV)*

When a person dies who impacted the lives of many people, we often hear, "They left big shoes to fill." This is currently the case with Jack because he was always a pillar in the community, in his church and especially in his family. He may have left "big shoes to fill" but he also left great footsteps to follow. I am talking about the legacy he left.

> **Children are a heritage from the LORD, offspring a reward from him. Like arrows in the hands of a warrior are children born in one's youth. Blessed is the man whose quiver is full of them. They will not be put to shame when they contend with their opponents in court.**
>
> *Psalm 127:3-5 (NIV)*

I admired how Jack worked hard and played hard and he always made time for his family. He loved it most when they were all together and provided opportunities to make that happen. I had never seen a father do anything like this to this extreme. Whether it was bowling, hunting, boating, taking vacations, going to the movies or just out to eat as a family, he loved having them all together. He placed great value on them and loved them big.

I learned from him early on that my family was my greatest possession outside of my relationship with the Lord, and I still hold firmly to that today. We did not do many family activities to bond us like the Dudleys when I was growing up, and we did not spend a lot of time together like Jack's family did and still do. When I eventually made a family of my own, I followed Jack's example and created memories with my family that would last a lifetime. My children look forward to those times also, but I think I look forward to them the most.

To impact the life of your family it will
require that you be intentional.

I grew up in a family that fought a lot and honestly did not really like one another or ever really want to be together. It was normal to get offended, fight and go years without speaking to one another. I never saw this in Jack's family. While there had to be problems at times, unconditional love and forgiveness always prevailed and love covered whatever took place.

I learned a few things from the legacy that Jack and Peggy created and Jack left. First, to impact the life of your family it will require that you be intentional. Family and legacy like this do not just happen on their own. It takes fathers and mothers who are intentional about staying in relationship with their grown children, their spouses and grandchildren and to continue to model love, faithfulness, integrity and generosity.

Second, it takes an investment of time and resources to have a close-knit, God-fearing family. It takes creativity and thought to figure out ways to bring your family together to be able to love, enjoy and be an influence in their lives.

I HAVE LEARNED about the importance of celebration. Birthdays, graduations and weddings are a big deal to those within a family who have reached a certain milestone. We must press pause in life and love them. Life is short and time goes by quickly. Cherish your family, make a big deal about little things and show them you love them and care.

> Jack came up to me and hugged me and told me he was proud of me ... and slipped me a $100 bill as we jumped in the car to leave.

I remember on my wife's and my wedding day how Jack and Peggy and their family took time out to celebrate with us and love us. When Gina and I were leaving the wedding, Jack came up to me and hugged me and told me he was proud of me ... and slipped me a $100 bill as we jumped in the car to leave. I still remember how special it felt for someone to do that and be so generous to us. I had never experienced that feeling before. To think that I meant that much to someone else was overwhelming. It was the kind of thing a father would do, and Jack did that for me. I purposed in my heart that day that I would do that for someone else one day. I have done it many times, even slipped the $100 bill to Jack's grandson, Justin, at his wedding.

When celebrating the holidays, take time to do things out of the ordinary together. This makes memories that will be cherished forever. Jack and his family did this well, and his family are still doing it without him. I think they find comfort in his absence knowing that he would be so happy that they are together having fun and doing whatever they are doing. Togetherness is what makes any celebration. We must create times of togetherness.

> No matter the age, any time we take time or do something for someone, it speaks love and lets the person know they are valued.

Taking time to celebrate is a big deal to kids and is a great opportunity to encourage them and leave an impression on them. No matter the age, any time we take time or do something for someone, it speaks love and lets the person know they are valued. I am thankful for the times when others have been there for me.

THE GREATEST THING any father or mother can do is pass on their faith. Leave faith footsteps. If church is not a priority to parents, it will not be a priority to their children. What one generation does in moderation the next will do in excess.

If the things of God are somewhat important to

parents, then the things of God will be less important to their children and not important at all to their grandchildren. I read an article that stated when a mother comes to Christ, her family will only join her at church 17% of the time; but if a father comes to Christ, his family joins him 93% of the time.

> Jack was a big giver and knew the principle of tithing and investing in the ministries of the church and missions.

The influence of the father as the spiritual leader in the home matters. It is important that fathers make church a priority if they ever want to pass their faith along. Jack made church a priority and attended regularly. His spiritual legacy of faith is something that will be carried on from generation to generation. I want that for my family as well.

JACK WAS A BIG giver and knew the principle of tithing and investing in the ministries of the church and missions. He and Peggy always served and supported their pastors in a great way. I see this same support continuing as their daughters and their spouses do the same thing and follow in their footsteps.

In my own life I see this in my legacy as my two older children are in ministry working for the Lord and growing in their faith journey, all because Gina and I have been faithful and made God a priority in our home.

My own legacy in this area of my life is a reflection of Jack's legacy and others who lived this example before me. John Maxwell wrote in his book, *The Twenty-one*

Irrefutable Laws of Leadership:

"A legacy is created only when a person puts his organization into the position to do great things without him."

This is what Jack did, in his family and in his business, and I plan to do the same. Jack was a successful businessman and could always make things happen. He was a producer and had the blessing of God on his life and in his business ventures.

I have seen this pass on to his daughters and sons-in-laws as they too have been successful in business. When we put God first, great things happen.

All of Jack's daughters married wonderful, Godly husbands and have wonderful children and even grandchildren of their own. There is a wonderful heritage in the Lord in the Dudley family. Jack's quiver was not only full but overflowing with blessings.

IT'S NEVER too late to start leaving a legacy that counts! It is never too late to leave footsteps that are worth following!

His mercy extends to those who fear Him, from generation to generation.

Luke 1:50 (NIV)

Jack left big shoes to fill when he left this world, but he also left big footprints because he left a big impression on the lives of everyone who had the honor of knowing him. I am just one of many who can testify of what a remarkable man he was. He had so many friends and touched so many lives. His legacy will continue throughout his family for generations to come. Jack feared and revered the Lord, and because of his faithfulness to God, he is in heaven today and has left a legacy worth repeating.

> I am forever grateful to Jack and Peggy Dudley for showing me what a family looks like and opening their hearts to a young man who had a lot to learn.

His legacy will continue even within my family as I continue to follow his example of what family looks like and leave a legacy for my children and grandchildren to follow. I am forever grateful to Jack and Peggy Dudley for showing me what a family looks like and opening their hearts to a young man who had a lot to learn.

I am thankful for the example of many men and their families that the Lord placed in my path to teach me things I needed to know. The Dudleys are at the top of this list, a wonderful family, and I attribute that to the fact that Jack was their patriarch. I love all of them so much and am thankful that they loved me and showed me what a healthy, Godly family looks like. Jack taught me about family and lived his life in such a way that you would want to follow in his footsteps.

Chapter 6

Love & Loot

Robert Hogan

WHEN I WAS at youth camp around the age of 14 or 15, I felt the Lord calling me into ministry. I had a lot to learn and there was still tremendous brokenness inside of me from things that had happened in my childhood. I wondered how God could use someone like me to do a work for Him. The truth I hadn't yet learned was that God does not see us as broken. He sees us fixed and visualizes potential in us even when we can't see it in ourselves. He is known for using the unlikely and broken to do great works for His Kingdom. Thank God we don't have to be perfect for Him to do a work through us as He completes a work in us.

The year was 1994, and I had taken a position on staff at a church in Spring, Texas, for a pastor named **Robert Hogan**. I am thankful that he gave me a chance for the sixteen years I was on staff there. I learned so much in my tenure there, but looking back on what I learned from him, I can narrow it down to two very important things: love and loot. What he taught me about them changed my life.

Now I know there are many different meanings of the word "loot" but the titles in each chapter of this book have two words, and they both begin with the same letter. This chapter begins with "L" and for that reason I chose the word "loot" to stand for money. I'll mostly use the word money for the rest of the chapter.

LOVE AND MONEY are both important in life. We all need love, and we all need money. I needed to learn about both and what God had to say about them. God placed me in the path of Pastor Robert Hogan to teach me.

Let all that you do be done in love.

1 Corinthians 16:14 (ESV)

Robert taught me how to **love people**. He is not just a teacher or speaker, he is a pastor who truly loves people and he does it well. When I first felt the call of God on my life to go into ministry, I thought I could never preach. Most of the preachers I had heard speak all yelled, screamed in the microphone, shook their heads, jumped up and ran around while they preached. It wasn't until I met Robert that I realized that not all preachers have to do that, that God could use a gentle-spirited man or woman to preach His Word, lead others to Jesus and pastor a church. Robert Hogan is a gentle, Holy Spirit-filled man.

Like Brother B and Margie, I saw the fruit of the Spirit in the lives of Robert and Brenda Hogan. From the beginning of my time working for them, they welcomed me and made me feel like I was a part of their family. They believed in me and saw something in me that I could not see in myself, and they invested in me as part of their staff.

I was first hired as the assistant children's pastor, then moved to children's pastor, then to fine arts pastor and became assistant to the pastor before leaving and planting the church where I am now lead pastor. I feel like God used my time there in various positions to prepare me for planting a church so that I could understand the many facets of church leadership and be able to relate to how to operate a church. I am blessed to have had this training ground.

I never met a shepherd who loved people like Robert does, and his love for God and other people was something I wanted and felt called to. I also knew that if I was ever going to be successful in ministry, I needed to love people effectively so they could see the love of God through me. Ministry is loving people, and if you don't love people, they will never see Jesus in you. The love of God is something everyone sees quickly when they meet Robert.

> **By this everyone will know that you are my disciples, if you love one another.**
>
> *John 13:35 (NIV)*

The way we love demonstrates who we are and who God is. The way we live out love reflects the gospel and the transforming power of the cross.

Robert loves to celebrate people's victories in life and always goes out of his way to be there if possible. He never wants people to walk through a valley alone. Early on, I saw how he loved people who were hurting. I was able to go on hospital runs with him and watch the way he visited and prayed with people who needed God to intervene and bring healing. I watched him sit with families while their loved ones were in surgery, and he celebrated their good reports and wept with them when the news was negative. He taught me that most of the time it meant more to people to just be there, that presence was what meant the most, instead of always needing the right words to say. He taught me to just be a willing vessel and let the Holy Spirit lead me. When the news was negative, he offered hope from scripture. He would speak from his heart and declare it from his lips at just the right time.

I also remember him saying to me that when loving hurting people, to just go and do it. The Holy Spirit would do the work. He encouraged me that the right words would come to my mind at the right time.

For the Holy Spirit will teach you at that time what you should say.

Luke 12:12 (NIV)

We don't have to have everything all figured out before we go and minister if we are led by the Spirit, we just need to go and love, and He will take care of the rest. It is God's work, not ours. We are just the vessels He uses.

WHEN PEOPLE lost a loved one, Robert was always there. If he could help, he would, and he wanted them to know God was there and that they were not alone. I have been with him when he has been with people who have gone home to be with the Lord; and walked with him alongside people who have experienced gut-wrenching loss in their lives. His example prepared me for the days ahead when I would walk with those in my own church. I have asked myself many times when walking through valleys with people, "What would Robert do?" Robert would just love.

The Bible says we are to love others the way God loves us. We are to love the family of God.

> ***Dear friends, let us love one another, for love comes from God. Everyone who loves has been born of God and knows God.***
>
> *1 John 4:7 (NIV)*

Robert did this, and from his example I learned how to love like Christ. He showed me how the Heavenly Father loves people by the way he loves people.

Robert went out of his way to attend funerals. He taught me that people need to know they are loved when they are hurting more than at any other time. I officiated at funerals with him where we sometimes fulfilled unusual requests of people to honor their loved ones.

Robert also taught me to love people even when it wasn't convenient. It reveals that God cares and will go to great depths to show them His love. On one occasion, we set a record driving to Oklahoma City from Houston in five hours for a memorial service at a university for a family who had lost their granddaughter while away at college. I learned how to shepherd the flock well from him and love people in their time of loss.

Robert went above and beyond to make sure people knew they were loved. It was not unusual for him to wake up before dawn and drive to the hospital to pray with someone before their surgery. It was not out of the ordinary for him to purchase food and deliver it himself to a family who suffering loss or just coming home from the hospital. There were even times when he would forgo family events and trips because someone was suffering great loss in the church. He taught me that loving people requires sacrifice. As I learned to love people under his guidance, he shared that his trust in me to love the people in his absence allowed him to occasionally take a little time away from his flock. I was glad I could provide that for him.

Greater love has no one than this, that someone lay down his life for his friends.

John 15:13 (ESV)

The calling to love is costly and requires sacrifice. Just as Jesus literally laid down His life for us, ministry requires that there are times that we must lay down things in life for the sake of loving others and sharing the gospel.

ROBERT LOVED all people and not only those in his congregation. He loved the church abroad but also the lost who needed Jesus. He had a heart to reach lost people, and I did too. Both of us wanted to share the love that we had found with those in our community. We did that for many years during the Christmas season.

God laid an idea in my heart to do something big for Him in our community. I wanted to initiate a Christmas outreach for the six weeks leading up to Christmas with the choir, drama and arts department to tell the story of Jesus to allow the lost to find salvation. When I shared it with Robert and told him how big it was, he did not look at me like I was crazy or kill my dream. He reminded me that if it was God, then God would provide if He wanted it done. He also prayed with me about it and reminded me that the funds to do such a thing might seem like a lot to me, but it was nothing for God.

Shortly after I shared this with him, he called to tell me that God had provided by means of a businesswoman in the church whose CPA had told her to give the exact amount we required for the outreach. She needed to donate to a non-profit for tax purposes, and we needed the money she had to give. We celebrated and thanked God. We remained involved in this outreach for ten years, and we saw thousands accept Jesus as their Savior and come to know God's love. During those years, we also presented many illustrated sermons to share the love of God with others who were lost.

> **Declare his glory among the nations, his marvelous works among all the peoples!**
>
> *Psalm 96:3 (NIV)*

Heaven only knows the impact of the love we shared in the community through the arts over the years. All the glory belongs to God!

I ALSO LEARNED a tough lesson about love while in ministry. When you love hard you hurt hard. I have witnessed Robert love people even when it was painful. Pastoring is tough, and when you invest years into the lives of people and they end up leaving for no reason or disappear because they have taken up offense, it hurts.

I have experienced this many times while pastoring and have learned that it is part of the price for leadership. From watching Robert handle this for years, I have learned that you love them while you have them, and you love them when they leave. You love them no matter what and in the same manner that God loves them. I have also had to remind myself not to take it personally when people leave, even though it is hard not to. I remind myself that I made a difference for a season in the lives of those who have left, and that my love and labor were not in vain.

So, my dear brothers and sisters, be strong and immovable. Always work enthusiastically for the Lord, for you know that nothing you do for the Lord is ever useless.

1 Corinthians 15:58

I have not always handled the "loving them when they are leaving" thing like I should, but I am getting better as I grow daily in the Lord and understand that this kind of pain comes with my calling.

I was blessed to experience Robert's ministry and learn many things from him, but the way he loves people is something I have modeled in my own life, and I have been able to impact many lives from the lessons he taught me. Robert has been a ministry father to me, and for that I am grateful.

ROBERT TAUGHT me about money and how to be a good steward.

For the love of money is the root of all kinds of evil. And some people, craving money, have wandered from the true faith and pierced themselves with many sorrows.

1 Timothy 6:10

On a long road trip, Robert and I playfully spent hours talking about all we would do if we won the lottery and all the people we would help with the funds. We concluded it was unlikely to ever happen for us, because you must play the lottery in order to win, and we wouldn't play. We even questioned that if someone in the church won the lottery, would we accept the tithe from it? Robert concluded that we would because *"the devil has had that money long enough."* My mom played the lottery and promised me if she won, she would give me some "loot," and I promised Robert if she did that, I would pay off his mortgage. I have many fun memories with him and still look back on some of the things we witnessed, went through and dealt with and laugh.

When we put money before God, we will lose out in the end.

The reference to money in 1 Timothy 6:10 can at first sound confusing to people. It is not saying that "money" is evil. but that the "love of money" is the root of all kinds of evil. Money can become a god to people, and people who love it more than God can and have done some crazy things because of it. When we put money before God, we will lose out in the end. We all have to have money to live, but when God is first in our lives and we live according to what He says about money in the scriptures, we can rest in the fact that He will provide all the resources we need and even bless us with extra handfuls.

> God placed Robert in my life to direct me and teach me in this area.

Robert helped me understand what the Bible had to say about money. People don't like to talk about it, especially in the church, but the Bible mentions money over 800 times. Money and possessions are the second most referenced topic in the Bible. Nowhere in scripture is debt viewed in a positive way.

Robert taught me about tithing, the blessing of giving and being a good steward with money, and gave me advice in my own finances that I have applied to my life. His lessons are still a blessing to me today. A young man needs financial advice, and God placed Robert in my life to direct me and teach me in this area. One of the things he often said was, "You can't outgive God." I have found that statement to be true all my life. Whether it be monetary or not, He is faithful to provide all we have ever needed.

And my God will meet all your needs according to the riches of his glory in Christ Jesus.

Philippians 4:19 (ESV)

The first thing I had to learn was that everything belongs to God! When you grasp this truth, you understand that all we have in life, whether monetary or otherwise, comes from Him, and He entrusts us to be good stewards with it. This is something Robert frequently preached about, and the church was always blessed because he did.

HOW YOU HANDLE money reveals volumes about your priorities, loyalties and affections. In fact, money directly dictates many of the blessings you will and won't experience in life. When you grasp this truth, you will begin to understand that all you have comes from Him, even money, and that He has entrusted you to be a good steward of it.

> Robert and Brenda have always been
> faithful with their tithes.

Several years ago, when I first set out to plant the church I now pastor, I read somewhere that the number one reason the unchurched do not like to attend church is that they think that all the church wants is their money. That is just an excuse. If giving is tied to receiving blessings, a pastor would be doing his congregation an injustice for not preaching about tithes and offerings and keeping them from the blessings associated with it.

Anyone familiar with Robert knows that he understands and lives under God's blessings because he and Brenda have always been faithful with their tithes, offerings, missions and giving to ministries within and outside of the church. I learned this truth from Robert, and Gina and I, like them, give above and beyond what is required because we learned that we can't outgive God. God also gives in ways besides money. He causes extra blessings of time, service and even prolongs the lifespan of items we use daily. God divinely intervenes in a supernatural way. There have been times in my life when funds were short, and someone would thankfully call us out of the blue and invite us out or over for dinner. God is faithful and takes care of His children. Robert has shared many stories like this throughout the years.

PEOPLE HAVE many different thoughts on the principle of tithing, and I have had a few of my own over the years. The first principle we look at when giving to the Lord is that of first fruits, which is the tithe. It is also called the principle of the firstborn.

> When Jesus redeemed us by His sacrifice, He bought us back for God and paid for our sins.

We tithe because God tithed. Jesus was God's firstborn and only born. Jesus was clean, perfect and unblemished in every way. When Jesus redeemed us by His sacrifice, He bought us back for God and paid for our sins. He was the spotless lamb, God's perfect firstborn. Jesus was literally God's first fruits offering.

In a very real sense, Jesus was God's tithe.

> *The next day John saw Jesus coming toward him and said, "Look, the Lamb of God, who takes away the sin of the world!"*
>
> *John 1:29 (NIV)*

According to Old Testament law, the firstborn was either **sacrificed or redeemed**. Jesus was sacrificed and He redeemed us as a first fruit tithe on our behalf.

God gave us His tithe in faith before we believed.

> *But God demonstrates his own love for us in this: While we were still sinners, Christ died for us.*
>
> *Romans 5:8 (NIV)*

We must give our first fruits offering, our **tithe** to God. God gave us His tithe in faith before we believed.

In much the same way, before we see the blessing of God, we are to give in faith. The principle of the first fruits is powerful. What we give to God we don't lose, because He redeems it for us. But what we withhold from God, we will lose. We tithe because God tithed to us when He offered Jesus. The first belongs to God, whether it be our time or our finances.

Tithing is really giving our first to God. It is saying: *God, I give to You first and trust that You will redeem the rest.* We tithe because God is first. A tithe is the first ten percent of our earnings and increase. When we don't tithe first, we put other things before God. When this happens, those things and even our money becomes our God.

You shall have no other gods before me.

Exodus 20:3 (NIV)

Tithing is a heart thing. You can't put money before God. When we choose to withhold the tithe, we are putting more faith in the dollars than we are the Provider of our dollars. He is our source.

When we tithe our first fruits to the Lord, we give to Him in faith trusting that He will provide even before we know if we will have enough. When we don't give to God first, we are placing and prioritizing other things before Him, and those other things become our god.

> As God's people, the first part of our week should be given to worshipping Him.

Faith is precisely what tithing requires. It is giving God our first fruits in faith out of our love for Him and our obedience to Him.

Coming to church the first day of the week is a way of giving the Lord the first of your time. As God's people, the first part of our week should be given to worshipping Him.

I wish I had a dollar for every time I heard Robert quote this next passage:

"Will a mere mortal rob God? Yet you rob me. But you ask, 'How are we robbing you?' In tithes and offerings. You are under a curse—your whole nation—because you are robbing me. Bring the

> **whole tithe into the storehouse, that there may be food in my house. Test me in this," says the Lord Almighty, "and see if I will not throw open the floodgates of heaven and pour out so much blessing that there will not be room enough to store it."**

Malachi 3:8-9 (NIV)

God makes it clear that if we keep the tithe for ourselves, we are robbing Him. We are stealing from God! Many Christians overlook this scripture and explain it away. Some say it is for the Old Testament and not for us today, but in the verse right before this, in the same chapter, it says:

"I the Lord do not change."

Malachi 3:6a (NIV)

The tithe, the firstborn, and the first fruits all belong to the Lord. This is not the Law of Moses! It is an unchanging principle established by an unchanging God.

Many people live without blessing as a direct result of stealing from God. They struggle through life financially and have conflicts in their marriage and strife in their homes. They never figure out that the firstborn, first fruits and tithes belong to God.

I believe most Christians are not living under the blessing they could have because of their lack of knowledge of the tithing principle.

Honor the L<small>ORD</small> with your wealth, with the first fruits of all your crops; then your barns will be filled to overflowing, and your vats will brim over with new wine.

Proverbs 3:9-10 (NIV)

Tithing in the Lord's house involves honoring the Lord with our possessions and with the first fruits of all our increase. If you don't work, you do not have increase. If you work, then you tithe on the amount you receive.

In the Old Testament, people were primarily farmers. They raised crops and animals. They tithed from their first fruits and firstborn first. No matter the form of God's provision, we are to honor Him with our first fruits. When we do, the blessing barn is opened to us and our barns will be overflowing.

God showed me that it was not my money but His provision that provided me work.

The first portion is the redemptive portion. The first portion you give has the power to redeem the rest. When we tithe, we stretch the rest and the rest is blessed. This was hard for me to understand when I first gave my life to Christ. I thought, "I work hard for my money," and then God showed me that it was not my money but His provision that provided me work and allowed me to be healthy to work. The principle of putting God first and the principle of faith initiates the blessing.

Something I heard years ago and truly believe is that if God doesn't have your pocketbook, He doesn't have your heart. Let that sink in. I have witnessed many people who desire to serve the Lord and know Him in a greater way but have never moved to a deeper level with Him because they have ignored His voice and disobeyed Him in tithing.

THERE IS A TEST in tithing. The number 10 represents testing throughout the Bible. God tested Pharaoh's heart 10 times; there are 10 commandments; God tested Israel 10 times in the wilderness while they wandered around. God tested Jacob's heart 10 times while he was working for Laban. Daniel was tested 10 days in the first chapter of the book of Daniel. In the New Testament, 10 virgins had their preparedness tested. There are 10 days of testing mentioned in Revelation 2:10; 10 is the testing number; and the tithe is 10%. Tithing is the only area in which the Christian is invited to test God.

> The tithe represents the ultimate heart test, challenging the heart of the believer.

Malachi is the last book of the Old Testament. I believe God placed this principle in the perfect place, for we find it in the book of the Bible bridging the gap between the old covenant and the new covenant.

Tithing is truly a test. The tithe represents the ultimate heart test, challenging the heart of the believer. Do you pass the tithe test? When we give our first ten percent to the Lord, the rest is blessed. 90% blessed goes a lot further than 100% cursed. I believe this so much that when I teach it, I offer a money-back guarantee for those in my congregation who will try it for 90 days and see if it works. I have never had anyone come back and ask for a refund. I have had many say that they received raises at their jobs, were refunded money unexpectedly and when things were tight, had provision that could only come from God.

> "Watch the little money and the big
> money will take care of itself."

Robert instilled this principle in me long ago, and I am forever grateful. I have lived under the blessing most of my life and can attest that it works. I am thankful that he is so passionate about giving, and I believe he truly desires that God's people live under His blessing.

That is the desire of my heart, also. I could go on and on about the way God has blessed my life and finances from the teaching on this principle that I learned from Robert.

ROBERT IS a good steward and smart when it comes to finances. Some of the things he said and taught me have stuck with me and helped me financially be a better steward. He told me, *"Watch the little money and the big money will take care of itself."* This is so true. If we are careful to not spend money on things that are really not necessary, when we need to purchase something that we need, even if it costs a lot, the funds will be there.

Robert has been successful with real estate investments and shared with me the value in investing in rental properties. I have followed his advice, and God has used it to bless me beyond what I ever thought possible.

The financial records of our church are set up like he set up his church. We have a record of setbacks to make sure all funds are allotted correctly and for me to see clearly at all times exactly where we are financially. We also require that all checks have two signatures as a safeguard for accountability. These are good, wise practices for any church. I have shared these things with other church planters to help them get started right. These safeguards are part of being a good steward with God's money.

> "If we take care of the missionaries,
> God will take care of the church."

Our church is big on giving to missions partly because I saw Robert make missions a priority. I remember him telling me, *"If we take care of the missionaries, God will take care of the church."* I can attest that this is true.

I believe all the knowledge Robert has shared with me and others about money is a direct result of him putting God first in his finances. I am a blessed man for having taken his Godly advice and from sitting under his teaching on this subject from the Word of God.

I AM THANKFUL for all I learned from Robert and Brenda Hogan and for my time on staff with them. We have gone through some tough times and even had our differences, but we still love one another, and I choose to celebrate all the good things and God things we experienced as a team.

I could write an entire book about love. It might be endless because it is so multi-faceted and complex at different levels. God's love for us is so deep. But the main idea about love that I learned from Robert is found is this:

> **Jesus replied, "'You must love the L**ORD **your God with all your heart, all your soul, and all your mind.' This is the first and greatest commandment. A second is equally important: 'Love your neighbor as yourself.'"**
>
> Matthew 22:37-39

I could write chapter after chapter about tithing and giving and show you many more scriptures to try to convince you of all the blessings behind it. But the truth is we don't do it to be blessed, although that is a benefit. We do it out of love and obedience to God's command; because He is first in our lives; and because He has our hearts.

I want you to be blessed and not rob God, and He wants to bless you.

If you do not currently tithe, try it. Bring your first fruits of your increase to the Lord. I want you to be blessed and not rob God, and He wants to bless you. You must love Him more than money.

> *"No one can serve two masters. Either you will hate the one and love the other, or you will be devoted to the one and despise the other. You cannot serve both God and money."*
>
> Luke 16:13 (NIV)

All I learned from Robert has blessed me greatly. His example of love and teaching on what the scripture has to say about money pertaining to tithing and giving has forever changed my life, my ministry and the church body under my care.

Chapter 7

Discipline & Discipleship

Jim Clairmonte

IN THE SUMMER of 1992 is when my wife, Gina, and I took an interest in one another after a youth choir tour trip with our church. I was 25 and Gina was 19. Up until this time, I hadn't looked at Gina as a girl to date because she was still in high school, and I was older than her. Things changed on the choir tour when we started talking and I realized that she had now graduated and was heading to college.

Gina was born in Hawaii and grew up during most of her childhood in Okinawa, Japan. Under miraculous, God-ordained circumstances, Gina came to live in Spring, Texas, with a wonderful couple named **Jim and Joycelyn Clairmonte**. They opened their home to her and took her in as a daughter and taught her about the Lord, the American way of life and how to live according to the Word of God.

After I asked Gina out, she said she couldn't go unless I asked Jim first. I was a little shocked, because in the world I was raised in, I had never heard of this, nor had I ever done this in previous relationships. I thought you were only supposed to ask permission if you were asking for a girl's hand in marriage, not for a date.

Jim had strict rules for dating his daughter, and the more I thought about it, I appreciated that even though Gina was not his own flesh and blood, he took the responsibility of training her and protecting her seriously.

> I did not know what to expect, but what happened for the next couple of hours was nothing short of a Godly interrogation.

Gina was away at college at the time, and I went to visit Jim to ask if I could take her on a date. I did not know what to expect, but what happened for the next couple of hours was nothing short of a Godly interrogation. He asked me why I wanted to take her out, what I liked about her and a bunch of questions about what I believed dating looked like. I even got questioned about my knowledge of the Ten Commandments, because he wanted to make sure that the things of God were a priority to me and that I truly loved the Lord. I was working part-time at the church we all attended, but he was smart enough to know that just because you work for a church does not mean you are a fully devoted follower of Christ. The truth is, I was a devoted follower of Christ at the time, but the Holy Spirit still had a lot more work to do in me. The "fully" part of "fully devoted" wasn't yet there.

The day I met Jim to ask about dating Gina, I began a wonderful relationship with him, and God began to use him in my life to teach me things I needed to know, things that I have carried with me in my life and ministry that have made a huge difference. I eventually asked Jim for Gina's hand in marriage, and on May 21, 1993, Jim walked her down the aisle and gave her my hand in marriage. Gina is the best gift that God has ever given me.

> The two things I feel that I learned most from him involved Discipline and Discipleship.

I learned so many things from Jim over the next sixteen years that truly blessed my life, things only a Godly father could teach and that I needed to know to become a man of God myself, a husband for Gina and a dad to my own children one day. In finding Gina, I found a wonderful Godly father-in-law and friend.

JIM WAS A MAN of the Word, who lived by the Word and had the desire to help others develop a life-changing relationship with the Lord. The two things I feel that I learned most from him involved Discipline and Discipleship.

From the time I first met Jim, he encouraged me to read a chapter from Proverbs a day to find wisdom from the Word. Since there are only 31 chapters in Proverbs, it was easy to do, and it only requires doubling up at the end on months with fewer days. I begin to practice this periodically in my Bible-reading journey and still do this some today. I learned that the fear of the Lord is the beginning of wisdom and so much more during my journey through Proverbs. I learned from Jim the importance of ongoing spiritual disciplines in believers' lives. You will never grow in your journey with the Lord if you do not set aside and devote time in His Word and communicate with Him in prayer.

Have nothing to do with godless myths and old wives' tales; rather, train yourself to be godly.

1 Timothy 4:7 (NIV)

    I think the above verse above makes it clear that to become Godly we must undergo training. Although we can learn from others, the best training to become more like Jesus involves spiritual disciplines that we commit to. Jim set the example for me and encouraged me to grow in the Lord, but he could not force me. It was something I had to decide for myself. I am so thankful for the extra push that he always gave me and how he always asked me what the Lord was speaking to me about. I guess he knew that if the Lord was speaking and showing me things that I was having fellowship with Him and staying on the right track.

    Life is full of times of training and disciplines. Training and discipline are required in many areas of life to succeed. We study for all sorts of tests and even discipline ourselves to make our bodies do things physically in order to advance. When an athlete trains for a special purpose, their entire life can be under that discipline, including eating, sleeping, free time and their body. Every part of who they are requires constant work to prepare for the task. In a similar way, to train spiritually, we are to follow the example of Jesus who disciplined His spirit and practiced certain disciplines that helped Him follow the way of God.

Some Christ followers are willing to suffer in many ways for a job, sport or other activity, but when it comes to growing spiritually, they don't want to suffer in any way. Spiritual growth does not just happen on its own. We must "train ourselves" in the area of Godliness and allow the Holy Spirit to reveal truth to us.

> Spiritual disciplines take time and dedication to develop and require commitment, but the growth and rewards are worth it to know the Lord in such an intimate and personal way.

There are many obvious spiritual disciplines that are important. I saw them play out in the life of Jim, and they became a part of my life: Bible reading, prayer, worship, submission and service. Spiritual disciplines take time and dedication to develop and require commitment, but the growth and rewards are worth it to know the Lord in such an intimate and personal way. They are also needed to live an overcoming and victorious life in this sin-filled world.

Other than the obvious spiritual disciplines we all know of, there are several other disciplines I witnessed in Jim's life that impacted how I would live and act in the future.

THE FIRST DISCIPLINE is to listen. Be silent. Not only are we to be silent and listen to the Lord, but we need to learn to spend plenty of time before the Lord and not do all the talking. We must also listen to others and consider what God may be trying to speak to us through them.

Jim taught me to be a listener. In him I found years of experience about things I never knew anything about. You and I do not know everything. God desires to teach us so much, but we must practice a willingness to listen and learn. You become smarter from listening than talking, especially listening to God, but also from listening to other people.

> **But the LORD is in his holy Temple. Let all the earth be silent before Him.**
>
> *Habakkuk 2:20*

Jim had wise lips and spoke life. He was one that God could use to speak to anyone.

THE SECOND DISCIPLINE I learned from Jim has to do with seclusion. Another word for seclusion is isolation. The devil loves people to isolate for extended periods of time so he can work on their minds. This is not God's design. He wants us to seclude ourselves for short periods of time to instill truth in us so that we are able to listen to Him. We need to hear from the Lord and spend quality time with Him. To do so, you must learn to get away by yourself and shut out the world. The world around us is noisy and loud and has an agenda that is the opposite of the Lord's. Pressing pause and getting alone with the Lord to not only pray but listen is important. I found in these times that as

I read His Word and listened, He spoke to me about the things that were dear to His heart. Jesus did this, and I think it is important that we do so also.

> **But Jesus often withdrew to lonely places and prayed.**
>
> Luke 5:16 (NIV)

ANOTHER SPIRITUAL DISCIPLINE I learned from Jim is to rest. I think people in the world we live in miss this discipline. Jim was a hard worker and very successful in business, but there was a time in his life when he was so driven that he hardly rested, and it took a toll on him mentally and physically. He did not know how to relax, but after a breakdown, God did a work in Jim's life, and he became more relaxed and rested more. He enjoyed time with his bride, Joycelyn (that is what he called her), and with his family.

He encouraged and reminded me to rest and not be so driven with work.

Jim's breakdown was before my time, but he wanted me to learn from what he had gone through. He encouraged and reminded me to rest and not be so driven with work. I appreciated his advice and recognized that when I don't rest, running on empty makes me less productive, and my ministry and family suffer. I am more stressed and shorter with people. By the time I got to know Jim, he had learned this lesson and was able to rest more and value time with his family. I was blessed to be considered part of his family and have Jim and Joycelyn in my life. God was Jim's first priority, and he was chasing after Him more than money. We are commanded to honor the Lord's Day and rest on the Sabbath.

Remember to observe the Sabbath day by keeping it holy.

Exodus 20:8 (NIV)

I have learned that when I get weary, I can run to Jesus:

Then Jesus said, "Come to me, all of you who are weary and carry heavy burdens, and I will give you rest."

Matthew 11:28

THE FOURTH DISCIPLINE I learned from Jim has to do with thinking. Another word might be meditation. We must make time to think about what God's Word says and quietly consider the truth in a selected verse and how God wants us to apply it to our lives. The season we are in can affect the truth God wants to reveal to us, and when God speaks, I find that it is a timely Word. It hits me right in the place I am at, validates where I have just been or prepares me for what is about to come.

I don't know how many times I have felt the Lord step in and show or speak something to me, and I have thought, "I have no idea why you are showing me this," only to experience it a short while later. When that happens, He reminds me of how He previously revealed His truth to me. I realize God was already preparing me, meaning that God is already present in my situation and working out my problems. I can find rest in His peace because I can trust in Him.

Be still, and know that I am God! I will be honored by every nation. I will be honored throughout the world.

Psalm 46:10

O God, we meditate on your unfailing love as we worship in your Temple.

Psalm 48:9

I learned this and so much more from Jim, and I am grateful. He taught me the importance of self-discipline and spiritual disciplines, I think the self-discipline is easier when the spiritual disciplines are in place, because we have the Holy Spirit working regularly in us to reveal the things about ourselves that need to be submitted and surrendered to God.

If we are going to develop Christ-like character in our life, there are certain disciplines and habits we need to practice as part of that lifestyle. There is an old saying that says:

Sow a thought, reap an act. Sow an act, reap a habit. Sow a habit, reap a character. Sow a character, reap a destiny.

As we allow the Spirit to work and renew our minds, we will act in ways that are pleasing to God; and as we act in ways that are pleasing to God, we will develop habits that will develop Christ-like character in us. As we develop Christ-like character, we will become more like Jesus!

DISCIPLINE WAS the key to Jesus fulfilling the will of the Father and is the key to us becoming like Him.

> ***Even though Jesus was God's Son, he learned obedience from the things he suffered.***
>
> *Hebrews 5:8*

Jesus grew up in a normal earthly environment for his day. He learned like we learn. He was not born with scripture flowing from His lips when He spoke. He had to learn it just like we do.

> ***Jesus grew in wisdom and in stature and in favor with God and all the people.***
>
> *Luke 2:52*

Jesus grew in His learning and so must we. I am thankful that we are not alone in our learning. We have the Holy Spirit, and God places people like Jim in our lives with a heart to mentor and help us learn. Look around you. If you did not have a father or even a mother to teach you the things a parent should, you have a Heavenly Father who has placed someone around you to do so. When I realized this truth, I began to grow in many ways in my life.

Discipline and discipleship go closely together and are

derived from the same root word ***discere*** which means "to learn." We are all called to be Jesus' modern-day disciples, and we cannot be a disciple without learning discipline.

> Jim was always willing to help mentor and disciple anyone who was open and teachable.

From the core of who Jim was, he had the desire to teach others and help them learn. He had a heart for discipleship. He wanted everyone to reach their full potential in life both spiritually and in their careers. Jim was always willing to help mentor and disciple anyone who was open and teachable.

JIM AND JOYCELYN took time out together to help strengthen marriages and meet with couples individually and in a group to disciple them. Jim would also go once a month to the prison and help hold Sunday services for those men who were incarcerated, as he had a heart for the less fortunate and hoped that by investing in them that they too would experience the life change that Jesus had made in his life. His great love was going to the boys Juvenile Detention Center and talking to the boys to mentor them and show them the right direction to take in life. Jim and Joycelyn also opened their home to many who were in crisis to teach and mentor them and help them get on their feet. In my eyes, he was just passionate about helping others find Jesus and wanting to help people better themselves.

Jim pushed me at times to be better, even when I didn't want to receive it. I have always been cautious when I speak, and when I was in my twenties, I filled in for our senior pastor one Sunday. Jim complimented my presentation then followed his compliment with a "but." It seemed I needed to work on not using double negatives. He cautioned me that it would make the difference between speaking before a small audience or a large one.

Honestly, it hurt my feelings, but I soon realized he was right. I accepted that he had spoken out of love and wanted to see me succeed in every way possible. He even offered to send me to a class to help me become a better speaker. He wanted everyone to reach their highest potential.

> Discipleship is about becoming more like Jesus. That is our goal in spiritual growth.

Excellence was Jim to his core, and because people knew that he could be trusted, his opinion was welcomed. Whatever he had to say about a topic, you could bet it was probably right because his desire was always to do things God's way and teach others to do things God's way. Jim was transparent about his life lessons in order to help others.

THERE WERE MANY things I learned from Jim's transparency in sharing his life lessons. His passion to disciple and mentor others so often helped those around him grow in Christ. Discipleship is about becoming more like Jesus.

That is our goal in spiritual growth. Jim desired to facilitate that growth in people's lives. Pointing others to Jesus is something that Jesus Himself actually commands us to do.

> ***Jesus came and told his disciples, "I have been given all authority in heaven and on earth. Therefore, go and make disciples of all the nations, baptizing them in the name of the Father and the Son and the Holy Spirit. Teach these new disciples to obey all the commands I have given you. And be sure of this: I am with you always, even to the end of the age."***
>
> Matthew 28:18-20

Right before Jesus ascended to heaven, He gave His disciples this Great Commission. It is also ours.

The emphasis here is on making disciples, not just making converts. Leading others to find salvation in Christ is the first step in making disciples, but believers do not automatically become disciples. To become a disciple requires learning, and learning comes through discipline.

The word disciple means a learner or student. Not only is a disciple one who is a learner or student, but one who follows someone's teachings. This is why in the early church the disciples were called Christians, which means imitators of Christ. To be a disciple is to strive to be like Jesus. According to God's Word, the Bible, disciples will have certain characteristics:

A disciple of Christ remains faithful to His teachings.

> ***Jesus said to the people who believed in***

him, "You are truly my disciples if you remain faithful to my teachings."*

John 8:31

A disciple of Christ loves others.

So now I am giving you a new commandment: Love each other. Just as I have loved you, you should love each other. Your love for one another will prove to the world that you are my disciples.

John 13:34-35

It is important to understand that a disciple is one who wants to become like his teacher. Jesus sacrificed time and effort for His believers. Discipleship takes sacrifice. We should make every effort to spend time and get to know our brothers and sisters in Christ and be willing to experience life with them so that they can learn from us and become more like Jesus.

A disciple of Christ bears fruit.

When you produce much fruit, you are my true disciples. This brings great glory to my Father.

John 15:8

When Jesus says "much fruit" He is not talking about an occasional good deed, but a lifestyle which causes people to know and glorify God. True disciples of Christ live lives that bring glory to God. And when someone notices their good works, they give God all the glory that He alone deserves.

Jesus created the perfect pattern for discipleship that works! He chose twelve men and sacrificed by investing His time and energy to experience life with them. He desired to create disciples who would further the gospel message and create other disciples generation after generation who would do the same.

Jesus was a disciple of the Father Himself. He surrendered and was obedient to God's plan and came into the world to save it. Before He could save it, He had to create disciples that would carry on sharing the truth and the gospel message. Paul reveals Jesus' generational discipleship plan to Timothy:

> **You have heard me teach things that have been confirmed by many reliable witnesses. Now teach these truths to other trustworthy people who will be able to pass them on to others.**
>
> 2 Timothy 2:2

I have heard it said before, and I also believe it, but when you are looking for those to invest in as disciples, look for those who are FAT.

By the acronym FAT I mean to look for those who are Faithful, Available and Teachable. Discipleship is messy and takes substantial sacrifice and time. There is nothing worse than trying to disciple or mentor someone who doesn't really want to participate or isn't really ready to become more like Jesus or be obedient to His mission.

We find a great example of this in scripture when Jesus

called a man to be His disciple:

> *He said to another person, "Come, follow me." The man agreed, but he said, "Lord, first let me return home and bury my father." But Jesus told him, "Let the spiritually dead bury their own dead! Your duty is to go and preach about the Kingdom of God."*
>
> *Luke 9:59-60*

This man was basically saying, "Let me wait until my parents die and then I will come." He didn't want to cause conflict in his home. This shows how relationships can keep us from following the Lord. Perhaps it would take too much time away from the ballfield, the lake or other family activities. The man was obviously missing the "available" part of the FAT equation. He might have been teachable, but his unavailability would not allow him to be faithful.

Being a disciple of Jesus is not easy and will cause conflict in our personal lives. I have seen sold out followers of Christ face conflict in their families and in their friendships. As fathers, it is important as the spiritual leaders of our homes to instill the importance of making disciples in order for your entire family to understand the mission and stay on mission. The command to "go" is not optional. Jesus is counting on us to pass on the truth of the gospel and become a healthy disciple who creates other healthy disciples. Jim knew the importance of discipleship and taught us that by example.

Are you willing to risk conflict and be uncomfortable in your life to be a disciple of Christ? Living as a disciple and in a Godly way in an ungodly world will not be easy. The righteous ways of the Lord go against the ways of the world. As disciples we must be willing to suffer ridicule and persecution as we pass on the gospel message of Christ and even die for Him if need be.

JESUS SHARED some very heartfelt and compelling word with a crowd in Luke chapter 9:

> ***Then he said to the crowd, "If any of you wants to be my follower, you must give up your own way, take up your cross daily, and follow me. If you try to hang on to your life, you will lose it. But if you give up your life for my sake, you will save it. And what do you benefit if you gain the whole world but are yourself lost or destroyed? If anyone is ashamed of me and my message, the Son of Man will be ashamed of that person when he returns in his glory and in the glory of the Father and the holy angels. I tell you the truth, some standing here right now will not die before they see the Kingdom of God."***
>
> Luke 9:23-27

Jesus' method of discipleship worked. He invested and poured into the twelve and they did the same and so on. The message made its way to the Gentiles and down to us. We must pass it on. We must not be silent.

One thing that is so important when discipling others is that you are only going to be able to create disciples like yourself. It is important that you truly desire to be an imitator of Christ and strive to be obedient as you grow in

Him. You do not have to be perfect but fully committed to becoming all that He desires you to be. You don't have to have all the answers that those you are mentoring may ask, but you must know who and where to find the answers. As a person who disciples others, you must be faithful to God's Word and teachings; love others enough to share truth; and bear fruit for the Lord, so that others can see you as an example and imitate what they see.

> God did something extra special when He sent Jim and Joycelyn into my wife's life, and the blessing carried over into my life and into the lives of our children.

Jim was a great man to pattern my life after. As a young man growing in the Lord, I also wanted to be that kind of a man. Jim took discipleship, mentoring and teaching others the truth in the gospel seriously and did his best to pass on what he had learned. He disciplined himself to discipleship. I am grateful that my wife and I benefited from his efforts. Jim went to be with the Lord on November 7, 2008, and we miss him greatly. He impacted our lives, and we will cherish his memory and the example of Jesus that he set before us. He was a wonderful father-in-law and spiritual father figure to me.

God did something extra special when He sent Jim and Joycelyn into my wife's life, and the blessing carried over into my life and into the lives of our children. My children needed Godly grandparents, and they found that in Pepaw and Memaw Clairmonte.

Chapter 8

Consistency & Compassion

Curt White

MANY YEARS ago, when I was a teenager, I met a wonderful family at the church I was attending that impacted my life and my family in a special way. Little did I know when I met the White family how our paths would later cross in a more intimate way and how **Curt and Betty White** would become an important part of my life.

I met them in the 80s but did not really get to know them until the 90s when they started attending church in Spring. Our reconnection was instant, and we quickly formed a strong bond, one we still enjoy today.

I was missing a father figure in my life, and my kids were also needing the love of Godly grandparents to influence their lives. We found what we needed in Curt and Betty White. They had a surplus of love to give, and from the time they appeared in our lives over 27 years ago, they have provided consistent love.

Some of my greatest memories have been when we were together. We have laughed, cried and prayed together throughout the years and have been there for one another when we needed each other the most.

I AM A MAN who has been blessed to have many friends. They say you can count your true friends on one hand, but I have always felt blessed because I felt like I could count my forever friends on both my hands and my feet. I love people and love being with people, so I have many lifelong friends that I cherish deeply who mean so much to me.

Curt and Betty White are lifelong friends who have loved us and treated us like family. Sometimes God sends friends into your life that are consistent and there for the long haul, and He sent the White family to do just that.

God sent Curt and Betty into our lives to help us in ministry, support us and become a spiritual family to us.

Up to this point in my life I had a lot of people come and go. My family was not close knit, and there were many inconsistencies. Today they would be considered dysfunctional, a family where rejection was the norm. No one in my family had taken much interest in my ministry up to this point, making it especially refreshing when God sent Curt and Betty into our lives to help us in ministry, support us and become a spiritual family to us.

They were with us from the birth of our twins and have been there ever since. All four of my children love them dearly and look to them as grandparents, and the Whites love my children in return just the same.

My family is better because Curt and Betty White and their family are in it. I love their three boys like they are my brothers.

CURT IS GENTLE and full of love. He has been and is a stable figure in my life. We all need people who support us no matter what we are going through, someone that we know will always there, especially in ministry. Many people come and go in life, but few are always with you. Curt has always been there for me.

When I think of what I have learned from God placing Curt in my life as a father figure, I think of Consistency and Compassion.

> **So, my dear brothers and sisters, be strong and immovable. Always work enthusiastically for the Lord, for you know that nothing you do for the Lord is ever useless.**
>
> *1 Corinthians 15:58*

The dictionary definition for consistency is being in the habit of doing the same thing on a regular basis. Consistency is the act of living by the same principles. It is the practice of being the same when it comes to attitudes, behaviors, beliefs and characteristics. Curt's love for me and my family is consistent and something regular in our lives. He is not wishy-washy, and his love for me has never depended upon what I did or didn't do for him and whether he liked or didn't like what I did. His love was unconditional, much like the Heavenly Father's love for me. His consistent love did not waver, and that love was a great example of Father God's love for me.

When someone is consistent in whatever they do, others can depend on them. This is how I feel about Curt. I never had to worry about him saying one thing and then doing another. If he said he was going to do it, you knew it would happen. He was always willing to help in any way he could. He was dependable, open handed and always made me feel like it was a privilege to assist me when I struggled.

From Curt's example, I have become more consistent to follow through on my intentions and do what I promise.

A consistent person makes up his or her mind and sticks to what they say they will do (or not do) in an unwavering way. God is consistent with us in His love and provision, and He wants us to be the same with our commitment to Him and in our relationship with others, revealing to them the consistency of God's love in our lives. We are to be people who are not wishy-washy about things or wavering in our faith.

THE WORLD needs more people who do what they say and follow through. There are people who talk a good talk and even mean well but fail when it comes to really being there for others and doing what they offer to do. From Curt's example, I have become more consistent to follow through on my intentions and do what I promise.

There are many benefits of being consistent. People know what to expect; you are successful in achieving your goals; others know they can depend on you; you are looked at as someone dependable; and when we are consistent in our walk with the Lord, we are living in His blessing. Our faith requires us to be faithful.

God expects consistency from us because He is consistent. We can depend on God because He is consistent in what He says He will do. His plans are steadfast and firm forever. People can be inconsistent in many things, but God is never inconsistent in anything. What He promises He will do will happen.

> **For no matter how many promises God has made, they are "Yes" in Christ. And so through him the "Amen" is spoken by us to the glory of God.**
>
> *2 Corinthians 1:20 (NIV)*

God never changes. His love never changes and His Word never changes. That is a major sign of consistency. Because God does not change, He can be trusted. Inconsistent people are hard to trust. I have been blessed to have Curt in my life as someone I can always trust. His even-tempered, steady disposition is the same each time I'm with him, bringing stability to my life.

God is reliable. We can count on God to remain the same. He always remains constant in His love towards us. We can always know what to expect from God. We may not always know exactly how He is going to work, but we can be assured He is working, and the result will be good.

God's goodness is consistent. Curt is a lot like the Lord in this area. I am thankful that God placed Him in my life as it has tangibly helped me see His heart through Curt's heart.

THE BIBLE contains many scriptures and examples about consistency. There are three areas in which God expects consistency. God calls us to be consistent in our obedience and do what we say we are going to do. God expects us to be consistent in our faithfulness to Him in every area of our lives. God desires and expects us to be consistent in our relationship with Him.

Our commitment shouldn't change with the circumstances. When a person is consistent, they are also committed. Inconsistent people give up easily when things don't go well for them.

When people are rooted in life and grounded and consistent, they grow through the struggles instead of quitting and running.

The church is filled with inconsistent people. Sadly, when something goes wrong, they don't like a sermon preached or they take up offense, they are gone. It happens all the time. When people are rooted in life and grounded and consistent, they grow through the struggles instead of quitting and running from church to church hoping to find the perfect situation to meet their "needs."

The truth is, if the perfect church did exist, it would not remain perfect once someone showed up with inconsistent behaviors. What if I planted a tree in my front yard, but after a while, I decided it would look better in my backyard. Then, after a few weeks, I realized it would be better in the front yard. So, I replanted it in the front yard. Not only will that tree fail to flourish and grow, but it also will struggle to survive. Many people are like this about church and God. They decide to go to church, pray and read their Bible regularly for a short time and then uproot themselves and disappear for a few weeks or months. Then they come back again for a while. Then they go back to their old way of living in sin for a season. When this happens, they never grow spiritually because they have never been consistent and taken root anywhere. They've missed the opportunity to truly grow and produce fruit in their lives. Satan uses distractions and offenses to lead us away from our journey in the Lord, and if we listen, we become inconsistent and never spiritually mature.

This saddens me as a pastor, and I know it must break the Lord's heart. Jesus says to us:

Remain in me, and I will remain in you. For a branch cannot produce fruit if it is severed from the vine, and you cannot be fruitful unless you remain in me.

John 15:4

Be careful not to take the devil's bait. His ploy is to kill your faith. For spiritual growth to occur, we must remain in one place with unbroken fellowship with God and be faithful and consistent. When we do this, we will produce lasting fruit. Curt has been grounded and has served on the advisory council of the church I pastor since its founding.

GOD CALLS us to be consistent in our intimacy. Inconsistency kills intimacy with God and with people. The fact that Curt has been a steady and stable father figure in my life is the reason why we are so close. The more time I spend investing in my relationship regularly with the Lord, the more intimate my relationship with Him gets.

Consistency brings us close to God and close to others. Do you want to grow closer to God? Do you want to be closer in your friendships with others? Being consistent is the key to close relationships in our everyday lives and in our spiritual lives. Consistency in our relationship with God starts with simple changes that can make a big difference.

God wants to spend time with us daily. When we are regularly in God's Word, we will only grow closer to Him. Set aside a time to spend with God every day without distractions.

Come close to God, and God will come close to you. Wash your hands, you sinners; purify your hearts, for your loyalty is divided between God and the world.

James 4:8

If you are not as close to God as you want to be, then make time to get alone with Him. Make the commitment to spend time in His Word and in His presence on a regular basis. As I said in the previous chapter, spiritual disciplines are important, and you must be intentional to make them happen.

The consistency that Curt and Betty have given me in my life has taught me about the steadfastness of the Heavenly Father's constant unconditional love for me and

His promise to always be there for me.

> I have passed what I have learned from Curt to my own children.

I have passed what I have learned from Curt to my own children, as I have been there for them and have done my best to be someone they can always count on. Curt has been consistent in His walk with the Lord even through tough times. He knows the faithfulness of God, and that same consistent faithfulness is what he lived in his own life and showed to others.

> ***No man shall be able to stand before you all the days of your life. Just as I was with Moses, so I will be with you. I will not leave you or forsake you.***
>
> *Joshua 1:5 (ESV)*

GOD CALLS us to be consistent in our compassion toward others. Curt has impacted my life and my family through his heart of compassion toward others.

> ***Therefore, as God's chosen people, holy and dearly loved, clothe yourselves with compassion, kindness, humility, gentleness and patience.***
>
> *Colossians 3:12 (NIV)*

Curt has a big heart and really cares for people. He is not selfish. He puts others before himself. He has a genuine concern for other people. My family and I have been blessed to be recipients of his love and compassion for many years. It is the small things he does that not a lot of people take notice of or even know about that mean so much.

When my oldest son Sterling was little, he took to Curt and built a strong bond with him. All my children adore Curt, but Sterling at a young age liked to frequently go to Mimi and Poppa's house and had an extra special relationship with them. It was because of the compassion and love he felt from them. He knew, even at a young age, that it was authentic.

Sterling always knew he could count on Curt and still does.

Sterling always knew he could count on Curt and still does. He would call Curt from the church landline on Sunday mornings when he went in early with me and put in his order for breakfast. Curt would show up a little later and produce his order, even after I had already provided Sterling with breakfast. Curt always did and still does want to make sure that none of the kids are hungry, and if they are, he will take care of it.

Sterling knew how to work Curt, and Curt knew it, but because he loved him, he allowed it. This is just one example of how he has loved my family and impacted our lives. His compassion has been a steady foundation, and we needed his love.

COMPASSION is a characteristic of Jesus. All throughout the Bible, we see Jesus showing compassion for people around Him. Jesus healed those who were sick; He saved the woman caught in the act of adultery from being stoned; He befriended the wee little man Zacchaeus; He offered forgiveness to those who needed it; He showed compassion to the woman at the well and healed and helped those who crossed His path in need. Jesus' lifestyle was one of compassion. It was a part of who He was and a part of His mission.

Compassion wasn't something that Jesus did when people were watching. It was something He did because He loved people.

Compassion wasn't something that Jesus did when people were watching. It was something He did because He loved people. Jesus made a difference in the lives of people. In Mark we find a great example of just how compassionate Jesus was to people:

About this time another large crowd had gathered, and the people ran out of food again. Jesus called his disciples and told them, "I feel sorry for these people. They have been here with me for three days, and they have nothing left to eat. If I send them home hungry, they will faint along the way. For some of them have

come a long distance."

Mark 8:1-3

We know the rest of the story and the miracle that Jesus did where He fed over 4,000 men plus woman and children with 7 loaves of bread and a few fish, but in these first few verses in this story, you can feel the compassion and deep concern He had for these people. It moved Him to do something.

We are called to compassion like this as His disciples today. Curt learned this well.

COMPASSION prompts action. Jesus set for us a great example, and when we are moved by the Holy Spirit with compassion about a situation, it should cause us to act. The truth is compassion with no action is worthless because nothing happens and nothing changes. Jesus cares, Curt cared (and still does) and we need to care for people enough to be moved to do something about it.

Dear children, let's not merely say that we love each other; let us show the truth by our actions.

1 John 3:18

When a need presents itself in life, we can either ignore it or be part of the solution. We can either be the hands, feet and heart of Jesus and be moved, or we can move on. The compassionate love that God showed us when He took action and sent Jesus to the cross to die for our sins should be the driving force behind the compassion we act on in the lives of others.

The Holy Spirit does not point things out to us for us to feel pity for others. He points things out so that we will have compassion on others. Jesus is looking for people to be His solution to the hurting and those He puts in our path who need help and to be shown His love.

I needed to be consistently loved by an earthly father. I needed to know that someone tangible had compassion on me and was committed to always be there for me. God sent Curt to fulfill that void in my life, and his actions have brought healing to me and are a daily reminder that my Heavenly Father is always there and will help when I call on Him.

My family is better because the White family is in our lives. I hope this chapter encourages you to open your heart to the fatherless (and others) and help fill the void that may be there from missing family. I hope that you will follow the character of Jesus and be a consistent and compassionate person and make a difference in someone's world.

There is a world of fatherless children out there that could benefit greatly from having someone like Curt in their lives. Be a Curt to others and let them tangibly experience the faithful love and compassion of the Heavenly Father.

Chapter 9

Dedication & Devotion

Marty Burroughs

I KNOW THIS book is about the men that God placed in my life to fill the father void that was missing, but God is not limited to using individuals of a certain age to help others grow and learn. In this chapter and the next, I will share how God used two friends, one my own age and one younger, in my life to help me grow in my journey with Him. Both have impacted my life greatly. I am a better man because they have invested in me.

They are father-like brothers in my life.

EVERYONE NEEDS one long-term trustworthy friend that they can tell anything to. I have been blessed to have several friends like this, and **Marty Burroughs** is one of them.

Before I found the Lord, Marty was there. In fact, God used him to reach me for Him. I recently asked Marty about when he met me and whether he had seen me as an evangelism project. I was lost and needed Jesus badly, and I'm sure that was obvious even to a young teen boy. He told me that he did not. He saw a great guy who had a lot of potential and was fun to be around. I think the more he got to know me, the more he realized how lost I really was.

> Marty and I love each other like brothers, and it has been that way now for over 40 years.

We were young and both 14 years old when we met in the 9th grade. I sat by him at the Christian school we both attended, and we hit it off as friends right away. We were total opposites, and the only thing we really had in common when we first met was that we both liked to have fun. I shared with you in an earlier chapter that the first week we met, he invited me to his house for the weekend, and we have been the best of friends ever since. His parents became my spiritual parents. Marty and I love each other like brothers, and it has been that way now for over 40 years. God blessed me greatly when he allowed our paths to cross and we became friends.

I have many cherished memories with Marty and his family, and his wife, Tammy, is one of my closest, dearest and trusted friends. I love her like a sister. I tease Marty that I like her more than him. Honestly, though, they are my family and I love them dearly, and they both mean the world to me.

When I think of Marty and what I have learned from our

relationship, I think of Dedication and Devotion.

I AM CERTAIN that early in our journey Marty could have given up on me, but he didn't. I am convinced that the Lord had a plan and part of that plan was to teach him patience from having a friend like me to deal with. At the age when I met him, my insecurities were at an all-time high, and the private turmoil I was in made me an emotional mess at times. I shared in an earlier chapter how I hid my hurts and heartaches by trying to be funny. I did a pretty good job of it, I guess, but I needed the Lord to intervene and do something that only He could do in my life. I needed salvation and the Holy Spirit to clean up some things in my life. Marty was different from other friends in my life up until this point, and his example changed me.

> I knew that Marty was a good guy and I wanted to be his friend.

When Marty and I first met, I cussed regularly. He told me, "If you are going to hang around me, you can't do that."

I remember thinking, "Who does this guy think he is telling me not to cuss? I bet he doesn't think his poop stinks."

Since I cussed a lot, I didn't use the word poop.

I really didn't know any better. I was raised around that kind of talk, but I knew that Marty was a good guy and I wanted to be his friend, so I tried my best to adhere to his request. I still cussed some but not around him. I respected him and the fact that it was not something he did or wanted to do. I just thought maybe he didn't cuss because his dad was a pastor. I know now it was Jesus in him.

WHEN I THINK of my friendship with Marty, I am reminded of the relationship of Jonathan and David in the Bible. I think every man needs a Jonathan in his life, and Marty is my Jonathan. Everyone needs a best friend to hold them up when they can't do it themselves. People are made for relationships, both with God and others. We are not meant to walk in this world alone. Life is easier and better with a trusted and loyal friend by our side.

> Neither of us would be where we are today without the friendship that has made us better men, husbands, fathers, followers of Jesus and ministers of the gospel.

I'm not sure who said it first, but there is an old phrase that has been used by politicians through the years that reflects our friendship. The phrase is, "When you see a fence post with a turtle balanced on top, you know he didn't get up there by himself."

Marty was there and Marty is still here (although perhaps not on an actual fence post), and for that I am grateful. He is a dedicated and devoted loyal friend. His dedication to our friendship and devotion to me on my spiritual journey and to my ministry has blessed me and carried me through some dark days. He has helped me many times to refocus when I needed to stay on mission.

Neither of us would be where we are today without the friendship that has made us better men, husbands, fathers, followers of Jesus and ministers of the gospel.

> *Two people are better off than one, for they can help each other succeed. If one person falls, the other can reach out and help. But someone who falls alone is in real trouble. Likewise, two people lying close together can keep each other warm. But how can one be warm alone? A person standing alone can be attacked and defeated, but two can stand back-to-back and conquer. Three are even better, for a triple-braided cord is not easily broken.*
>
> Ecclesiastes 4:9-12

With a friend around, we can have a higher success rate in life. When we have a dedicated and devoted best friend who fears the Lord, we gain spiritual accountability as well as a great cheerleader in life.

When Elijah was by himself in the desert and he struggled with depression almost to the point of suicide, God sent Elisha to Him. When David gave in to lust and committed adultery, God sent Nathan to confront him and restore him. When John the Baptizer was isolated and alone in prison and started doubting that Jesus was the Messiah, Jesus sent a scripture through one of John's disciples to assure him that He was who He said He was.

James had and still has Marty (and Tammy) to talk him off the ledge and remind him of whose child he is. We all need a dedicated and devoted friend sent by God into our lives to speak truth to us when we most need it.

In my early twenties, I was pretty lost and messed up and not having an easy time finding my right path. I was working as an activities director at a nursing home and still living with my mom and stepdad. I liked my job and loved most of the crazy people I worked with, but I really hated going home every night. I looked for things to do to occupy my mind and my time. I'll spare you the details, but let's just say I needed Jesus really bad.

> They asked me one simple question:
> "What's it going to take to get you to
> fully commit your life to Jesus?"

During this time Marty and Tammy had graduated from Southwestern Assemblies of God University (SAGU), south of Dallas, gotten married and moved back to the area to join the staff at a church in Spring. I remember Marty and Tammy asking me to come over their house one night after I got off work. I found out once I got there that they had invited me over so they could have a "come to Jesus" meeting with me.

They asked me one simple question: "What's it going to take to get you to fully commit your life to Jesus?" They knew I needed help, and they were willing to step up and be the friends that I needed. I said, "I really can't explain it, but I dread going home every day. It feels like I've been in the sunshine all day and then I go home to darkness." My mom and stepdad didn't know the Lord at the time, and a demonic presence was so strong in their home that you could feel it.

Fortunately for me, Marty and Tammy had an unfinished garage apartment on the back of their house, and they had just received a new Discover card with a $5,000 limit. They committed to using the credit card to build out the apartment and move me in ... a generous act that saved me.

Marty asked his older brother Mike to come help us build out the apartment and, before long, Mike had it done. I moved in and quickly filled it with furniture. Real friends see you at your worst, still love you and call out the best in you! Thank you, Mike Burroughs, for being a big brother to me and building a place for me. Thank you, Marty and Tammy, for caring for me and for maxing out that credit card so I could have a home. I hope you've paid it off by now!

> I fell into a season of despair right before Gina found out she was pregnant with Brighten.

Not long after this, I was back in church all the time, helping out everywhere I could. Being at the church often and serving to the best of my ability is what opened up a door for me to join the staff at the church in Spring. It was during this period that I met and married Gina and our twin babies were born. Those were good days, but anytime you are doing something significant for the Lord, you can expect to be attacked.

I FELL INTO a season of despair right before Gina found out she was pregnant with Brighten. The depression was so severe that I could not get out of bed at times. The devil had really done a number on my mind, and he even used God's people to do it. During that season, I directed the choir on Sundays. I put on a happy face each Sunday, directed the choir that morning and afterwards left the platform to drive home and go to bed. I never considered suicide, but I did pray and ask God to take me home and remove the pain. Marty sat with me several times. He listened and spoke truth even though I could not hear it at the time. I eventually visited a wonderful counselor in Dallas who was able to help me. I realized afterwards just how devoted a friend Marty was to me during that season. He never gave up on me. Sometimes you just need to know you are not alone, and you need someone to listen and pray with you and fight the enemy with you.

> True friends uphold one another with love and loyalty.

Having the right friends is essential to your spiritual well-being as a follower of Christ. The biblical definition of a friend is someone who joins you on a journey as a devoted companion and guide. True friends uphold one another with love and loyalty. Ultimately, Gina is my very best friend, but we all need a friend other than our spouse to speak truth into our lives and love us no matter what. Another man understands the way a man can think, just as ladies can understand one another.

We see this kind of friendship in the Bible with David and Jonathan. Their friendship is what true brotherhood should look like between men who desire nothing more than to know God, serve God, please God and see Him glorified. After David defeated the giant Goliath in the book of 1 Samuel, in verse 18:1, it says:

After David had finished talking with Saul, he met Jonathan, the king's son. There was an immediate bond between them, for Jonathan loved David.

1 Samuel 18:1

Their immediate connection had to do with their mutual desire to see God be glorified. Jonathan was a dedicated and loyal friend to David. His father, King Saul, became jealous of David to the point of wanting to kill him. Jonathan was in a tough predicament, as his father wanted to kill his best friend. David found his life was in Jonathan's hands as Jonathan had to balance his loyalty to his father, to God, to Israel and to his best friend. David trusted in his friend to do the right thing before God and that Jonathan would not harm him.

Jonathan was a safe place where David could be vulnerable.

There are "friends" who destroy each other, but a real friend sticks closer than a brother.

Proverbs 18:24

We all need someone who will protect us and our reputation, that we can truly be ourselves with, a Jonathan of quality character, someone who loves the Lord and who will defend truth and who loves us for who we really are.

David trusted Jonathan's words. When Saul set out to

kill David, David knew he could trust his best friend's intentions and followed Jonathan's advice to escape the wrath of the king.

> *Saul now urged his servants and his son Jonathan to assassinate David. But Jonathan, because of his strong affection for David, told him what his father was planning. "Tomorrow morning," he warned him, "you must find a hiding place out in the fields. I'll ask my father to go out there with me, and I'll talk to him about you. Then I'll tell you everything I can find out." The next morning Jonathan spoke with his father about David, saying many good things about him. "The king must not sin against his servant David," Jonathan said. "He's never done anything to harm you. He has always helped you in any way he could. Have you forgotten about the time he risked his life to kill the Philistine giant and how the LORD brought a great victory to all Israel as a result? You were certainly happy about it then. Why should you murder an innocent man like David? There is no reason for it at all!" So Saul listened to Jonathan and vowed, "As surely as the LORD lives, David will not be killed." Afterward Jonathan called David and told him what had happened. Then he brought David to Saul, and David served in the court as before.*
>
> 1 Samuel 19:1-7

Jonathan put his life on the line for his friend, David. Jonathan stood up to his father who was king on behalf of David, and King Saul had a change of heart about killing David. True friends like this are hard to find, but David found a dedicated and devoted friend in Jonathan. I feel so blessed that God placed Marty in my path as this kind of friend and brother.

> Marty stood up for me and was willing to put his own reputation on the line to defend me.

I want to clarify that Marty's dad, Brother B, never set out to kill me, although there may or may not have been times when he might have wanted to when Marty and I did something stupid. But there were several times that I know of when Marty stood up for me and was willing to put his own reputation on the line to defend me and put in a good word for me. He believed in me early on, even with all my flaws, and saw the potential in me that God could use, if I surrendered my life to Christ and if someone was willing to give me a chance.

EVERYONE WHO knows me knows this, but I do not fit the typical preacher mold, mainly because of my upbringing. Not everyone was willing or anxious to embrace me in ministry at first. Marty did and was always willing to put in a good word for me and clear up any misconceptions about me that others might have had.

When God called me to plant the church I now pastor, things got pretty crazy. The devil was working overtime trying to stop God's plan to plant the church. There were many close to me that did not want me to step out and do it, mainly for their own selfish reasons. Marty believed in me and supported what I felt called to do. Someone told one of the officials at our denominational district office lies about how I was handling things with the launch of the new church. I got a call and told them it was not true. I don't think they believed me, but Marty knew the truth and spoke up to bring clarity to the situation. Some friends might have kept quiet or felt like it was best to stay out of the situation, but not Marty. Jonathan did the same with David when he spoke with the king, and I am thankful Marty did that for me.

In a sense Marty put his own reputation on the line for me and caused others to have a change of heart. For that I owe enormous gratitude to him for how he chose to see me (and all my flaws) and the work the Lord was doing in me through God's eyes and not through natural eyes. Like David and Jonathan, Marty and I had one thing truly in common. We both loved the Lord and more than anything wanted to please Him and bring Him glory.

> Jonathan ... helped David draw near to God when things in his life became difficult.

WHEN YOU read through the book of Psalms, you see many of David's writings. You can tell from reading them just how close he was to God. One main reason was because Jonathan had been in his life and taught and helped David draw near to God when things in his life became difficult. David learned to depend on God more than Jonathan, and we need to do the same.

> We all need someone to help us draw
> close to the Lord in difficult situations.

God placed Marty in my path as a spiritual father-like brother who was and is a dedicated and devoted friend. Marty loves me, teaches me and guides me as I continue to grow in the Lord, just as he did when we were younger. We all need someone to help us draw close to the Lord in difficult situations.

I heard once that we have three kinds of friends in our lives. Those who have a view, those who have a voice and those who have a vote. Those who have a vote are like Jonathan and Marty. You let them have a say that needs to be said, and you listen to them. There have been times in my life when Marty's council has gone against my emotions, but I have learned to trust his judgment and know that whatever he tells me is for my best interest. Marty and Tammy get a vote in my life!

DAVID, like me, had a rough and tainted past. I had a lot of baggage that needed to be dealt with. David was an adulterer and murderer. But God saw beyond his past and looked at his heart. David is not remembered for his past sins; he is remembered as a great king with a heart for God. Jonathan's influence in his life played a major part in how we view him today. Marty's influence has done the same in my life.

But God removed Saul and replaced him with David, a man about whom God said, "I have found David son of Jesse, a man after my own heart. He will do everything I want him to do."

Acts 13:22

Lord, may we *do everything you want us to do!* When a person is dedicated to another, it means they are committed to them. When a person is devoted to another, it means they are loving and loyal toward them. God is both these things to us, and these are both characteristics we find in Him that we all need to develop in ourselves.

When we truly embrace His love, we see His dedication and devotion toward us, and we realize the magnitude of it. When we think of how He sent Jesus to save us and redeem us from our sins, it becomes real to us. Only when this becomes real to us can we surrender and become like Him, dedicated and devoted to our Lord and to others. It is when we allow the Holy Spirit to work in us that transformation like this can happen. We love others like this because He loves us like this.

We love each other because he loved us first.

1 John 4:19

I am thankful that the Holy Spirit placed people in my path and did a work in their lives and used them to do a work in my life. Never forget that God uses people to accomplish His work in this world. Make yourself available and open your heart to let Him work in you and through you. I am thankful that Marty and Tammy Burroughs did, because my life is much better because they have been in it for so long and continue to be in it.

God has a Jonathan for every David, and God has a David for every Jonathan. We are not meant to walk alone in the Lord. I encourage you to seek out this kind of dedicated and devoted friendship with someone and also become the same kind of friend to someone. These kinds of relationships are God-ordained and God-ordered and are productive to bringing spiritual growth into our lives.

Here's a thought for you to consider:

To find this kind of friend, you must first be this kind of friend.

Chapter 10

Courage & Confrontation

Nathan Rouse

WHILE WORKING at the church in Spring in 2004, I crossed paths with a young man who would quickly become one of my best friends and impact my life greatly. His name is **Nathan Rouse**, and he and his wife Erin are very special to me.

    I think one of the reasons I was drawn to Nathan was because our backgrounds were similar. We did not grow up in God-fearing homes, but God directed our paths and placed the right people in our lives to reveal Himself to us. We were both called to the ministry and wanted to be used by the Lord to do great things for Him. We both disguised the pain of our past by trying to be funny and both wanted and needed acceptance from others. We both felt we had to perform for people's approval. While we were both at college years apart, we both got in trouble. (I had played a prank on my friend, Jeff, and put his and a girl's photo in the local newspaper announcing their engagement. I made it all up because Jeff had been leading this girl on. Long story short, I got probation at the college and had to write a ten-page paper on hazing.) Nathan has his own story about a few crazy stunts he performed while there as well. Feel free to ask him, but that is his story to tell, and I make no promises on his part.

NATHAN is a one-of-a-kind guy, and when you meet him, you know there is something special about him. He is gifted in music, drama and speaking, and is an author and most of all a courageous and honest friend who does not back down when it comes to confrontation. God uses him mightily to speak truth into my life in a way that is loving. He is nine years younger than me, but His wisdom far surpasses mine. That is makes him a father-like brother to me.

> It wasn't until I heard him share his testimony about his childhood that I realized just how courageous he was.

We both grew up in dysfunctional families. It wasn't until I heard him share his testimony about his childhood that I realized just how courageous he was. He had suffered abuse and was open to share with anyone who needed to talk about how God had brought him out of that darkness and into His light. God had done the same for me, and Nathan was the first person I shared my own story of abuse with. It set me on a new path of healing. Up until then, I had kept it hidden deep within because of the pain and shame it brought me to even think about it. God placed Nathan in my life for many reasons, but I learned from him how to face situations with Courage and not be scared to Confront others with truth instead of ignoring unpleasant situations.

> *As iron sharpens iron, so a friend sharpens a friend.*
>
> Proverbs 27:17

This shared bond of our similar pasts is why Nathan means so much to me. He is not afraid to sharpen me, but he does it in a way that I know he is sharpening me out of love. He desires nothing more for me than to see me succeed and overcome every obstacle the enemy has placed in front of me.

> *But that night the word of God came to Nathan, saying: "Go and tell my servant David, 'This is what the Lord says ...'"*
>
> 1 Chronicles 17:3-4 (NIV)

Nathan Rouse is like the biblical Nathan from Chronicles to me. Just as David had a Jonathan in his life, David also had a Nathan in his life. Jonathan and Nathan played important roles in David's life. Nathan Rouse is my biblical Nathan, and I am so blessed that I have him in my life.

I know I am different and have many flaws, but Nathan knows it also and is willing to call those flaws out. He is courageous and not afraid to confront my thinking or attitudes that are off or birthed out of emotion.

Nathan doesn't care if I get angry at what he is saying to me, because he is more concerned that I know the truth. We all need a Nathan in our lives, and I am thankful for mine.

> We all need a guy in our lives who is willing to be harder on our sin than we are.

In the story of David and Nathan in the Bible, we see this same kind of relationship play out. Nathan is a courageous prophet who is not afraid to confront wrongdoing. The prophet is not afraid to ask David the hard questions. We all need a guy in our lives who is willing to be harder on our sin than we are. We like to play down the things we have done and make bigger the things that other people do, but the truth is that sin is sin, no matter how big or little, and we need someone like Nathan to remind us of that and to keep us in check.

Nathan was attending the church I worked at, and we were preparing for a Christmas production. We were in chorography practice, and no one was listening. I lost my cool with the group and verbally let them have it. After the practice, Nathan took me aside and told me, *"You can't blow up like that. These people are giving of their time to be a part of this, and although you want excellence, you can't talk to them like that."* He was right, and I took it to heart from that day forward. He helped me to think and see things from the view of those in the chorography group, to see that they were volunteering their time to help minister. From that one "correction" from him, I learned to be careful when correcting and to do so in a way that encourages instead of tears down. I apologized to the group that day and thankfully nobody quit.

> **To learn, you must love discipline; it is stupid to hate correction.**
>
> *Proverbs 12:1*

To Nathan's credit, my friend had earned the right to discipline and sharpen me. I trusted him and knew that he would only tell me things because it was for my good and not because he was looking for an opportunity to point out what I was doing wrong.

If you are going to be a person in someone's life that sharpens them, make sure you are their trusted friend first. Discipling someone without trust is ineffectual. It will accomplish nothing.

IN THE BIBLE, the concept of correction and rebuke means confronting sin so that we feel the weight of its seriousness before God. When we let someone like a Nathan into our life, they help us recognize the need for change. Even though rebuke can get messy, and we don't like it, God says it is a good thing.

> **Take no part in the worthless deeds of evil and darkness; instead, expose them.**
>
> *Ephesians 5:11*

The exposure is painful, but I am thankful for friends like Nathan in my life who are not afraid to confront me when I am wrong. If we are going to grow in the Lord, we cannot resist a friend's willingness to be courageous and confront us and let us feel the conviction that the Holy Spirit wants to place on our hearts. Don't resist a trusted friend's willingness to speak up and speak truth into your life.

> Instead of confessing his sin and correcting it, [King David] devised a scheme to cover things up.

King David had a courageous friend in Nathan. When David gave in to lust and sinned with Bathsheba, the wife of Uriah, one of his soldiers, Nathan did not stay quiet. Even though David was the king, he spoke up.

David had gotten Bathsheba pregnant. Instead of confessing his sin and correcting it, he decided to cover things up. David called Uriah in from battle hoping that he would sleep with his wife and cover up the pregnancy. Things did not work out like he planned, so he decided to kill Uriah by sending word to his generals to put him on the front line. He was then killed in battle, and David took Bathsheba as one of his many wives.

David's scheme fooled everyone, and the people looked on him as a hero for taking Bathsheba as his own wife after Uriah's passing. God was not pleased, and He sent Nathan the prophet to confront him.

*So the L*ORD *sent Nathan the prophet to tell David this story: "There were two men in a certain town. One was rich, and one was* poor. The rich man owned a great many sheep and cattle. The poor man owned nothing but one little lamb he had bought. He raised that little lamb, and it grew up with his children. It ate from the man's own plate and drank from his cup. He cuddled it in his arms like a baby daughter. One day a guest arrived at the home of the rich man. But instead of killing an animal from his own flock or herd, he took the poor man's lamb and killed it and prepared it for his guest."

David was furious. "As surely as the LORD lives," he vowed, "any man who would do such a thing deserves to die! He must repay four lambs to the poor man for the one he stole and for having no pity."

Then Nathan said to David, "You are that man! The LORD, the God of Israel, says: I anointed you king of Israel and saved you from the power of Saul. I gave you your master's house and his wives and the kingdoms of Israel and Judah. And if that had not been enough, I would have given you much, much more. Why, then, have you despised the word of the LORD and done this horrible deed? For you have murdered Uriah the Hittite with the sword of the Ammonites and stolen his wife. From this time on, your family will live by the sword because you have despised me by taking Uriah's wife to be your own. This is what the LORD says: Because of what you have

done, I will cause your own household to rebel against you. I will give your wives to another man before your very eyes, and he will go to bed with them in public view. You did it secretly, but I will make this happen to you openly in the sight of all Israel."

Then David confessed to Nathan, "I have sinned against the L*ORD*."

Nathan replied, "Yes, but the L*ORD* has forgiven you, and you won't die for this sin."

2 Samuel 12:1-13

Nathan is the right choice for several reasons. He was already a trusted friend to David; Nathan was more loyal to God than to David; and he was courageous and careful in confronting David and communicating with him that God was not pleased with him. Nathan had no problem communicating the consequences of sin and grace, hope and comfort that God wants to give David.

Nathan says all this and commits to be his faithful friend to the end. Because of this David responds correctly and confesses his sin.

Wounds from a sincere friend are better than many kisses from an enemy.

Proverbs 27:6

A true friend does what is in your best interest whether you like it or not and whether you ask them to or not. A friend like Nathan is not afraid to tell you something that may hurt you in order to heal you. He or she will take the chance. A friend like Nathan knows you best because you let him into your world, and he or she knows your heart and you trust theirs.

A true friend like Nathan desires your friendship but is a better friend to God. His loyalty to God is greater than his loyalty to you or any other friends. Because of this, you can trust that whatever he tells you or advice he gives you, it is going to come from God's perspective and be correct.

A Nathan is more concerned about helping others to live in truth than losing their friendship. We all need a Nathan in our lives, but we all need to be a Nathan to the friends that God has blessed us with.

> **The human heart is the most deceitful of all things, and desperately wicked. Who really knows how bad it is?**
>
> *Jeremiah 17:9*

It is hard to see our own heart. It is not hard for a Nathan, though. As we open up and share our struggles, feelings and concerns, we reveal our hearts to others. I do this with my wife and in my conversations with friends like Nathan, and when I do, they keep me balanced.

David experienced pain for his actions. Even though God forgave him, the consequences for his sin remained. The consequences were personal and hurt, but they also had purpose. The pain must outweigh the pleasure to discourage us from going back to the sin. Sin can scar us, and it reminds us of its devastation and our need to repent.

The Nathans in our lives are there to warn us about the consequences of sins. They do not play down our sins but hold us accountable until we see that what we have done is sin and we repent. Once we do repent, they are there to offer us grace, comfort and encouragement.

Nathan was firm in his rebuke and quick to offer grace and a promise of eventual redemption. A Nathan understands that repentance results in forgiveness.

> **But if we confess our sins to him, he is faithful and just to forgive us our sins and to cleanse us from all wickedness.**
>
> 1 John 1:9

At the end of David's life, there was drama and political tension. The king felt helpless and weary. Nathan once again helped David lead the nation back into peace by making sure that Solomon would be crowned king to succeed him.

Nathan was a true friend to the king and loyal to the end. He stuck by him in good times and through bad times. He always spoke the truth and never became bitter toward David. Nathan knew David's heart, and David knew and trusted Nathan's heart.

> Because Nathan Rouse is like David's Nathan, he was quick to offer me grace and embrace me again like nothing had happened.

Sometimes I think we fear that the people who really know us will push us away. There may be a little truth to that for those who are not mature believers in the faith. But Nathan was mature and committed to God, and he was committed to God's truth being revealed. That is what prophets do, reveal God's truth.

The Nathan that God placed in my life has usually been right. He tells me some things that I don't always want to hear but need to anyway. Sometimes I don't like it, occasionally I resist at first, and then usually I take the advice and do what he says, because in the middle of the battle, I am too weary to think or figure it out and just have to depend on my Nathan to tell me what to do.

I AM BLESSED to have a friend that I can trust no matter what he says. At one point, I disagreed with him so strongly that I quit communicating with him for a season, yet deep down I knew what he said was right, and I repented and made things right with him. Because Nathan Rouse is like David's Nathan, he was quick to offer me grace and embrace me again like nothing had happened.

We all need fathers, father-like brothers, mothers, mother-like sisters and friends that God has placed in our paths and raised up to speak into our lives. We need to grow in the Lord and be that kind of person to others, to be a Nathan to them. God uses people like this in our lives to be His hand extended, to be the father that we need.

A Nathan sent from God provides the tough love that we need in order to grow. Identify your Nathan and don't resist what they have to say. Embrace them, because God sends them into your life to help you grow and make you a better person. Let them speak truth and life into your life. Be a Nathan to someone else. God has placed you in someone's life for you to disciple in His truth.

Chapter 11

Pursuit & Perseverance

Mike Allard

WHEN I WAS a teenager, my path crossed with a youth pastor who would eventually impact my life in so many ways. I would go to youth service with some of my friends across town, and that is where I met **Mike Allard** and his sweet wife Danielle, who I lovingly today call Nellie.

Mike is a wonderful pastor, teacher and compassionate storyteller, but over the years he has also become a trusted friend who has filled the father void spiritually in my life and who has always believed in me and taken time for me when I needed his help the most.

Mike served as our district youth director and did a fine job of it for over eleven years. He set the bar high for that position, and it was during those years that Mike became one of my heroes in the faith. Mike, like Marty, believed in me. He saw the creativity in me and knew that God could use it, so he put me to work. One summer when I was at youth camp with him, I felt God call me into ministry. Mike believed in me and encouraged me in my calling. He introduced me to a wonderful discipleship program for students called Fine Arts Festival. Mike got me involved at a district level and then put in a good word for me, and the leaders on the national level reached out to me and got me plugged in to help. I have now been involved with this ministry for over thirty years locally and nationally.

> Mike and I also have a creative side in common, and he recruited me to help with many illustrated sermons over the years at the youth conferences he hosted.

The Fine Arts Festival has played such an important part in my life and ministry and has impacted my children in a great way. I attribute their hearts for God and ministry to the fact that they grew up and were discipled through this student ministry program.

Mike and I also have a creative side in common, and he recruited me to help with many illustrated sermons over the years at the youth conferences he hosted. God used our efforts to impact the lives of students all throughout South Texas. I was and am always honored to be a part of anything he does, because his efforts are always to bring others to Jesus and bring glory to God. I think Mike was able to see my gifts, and he wanted to put them to use and help make sure I was using my creativity for the Lord.

God has given each of you a gift from his great variety of spiritual gifts. Use them well to serve one another.

1 Peter 4:10

I have learned a lot from Mike over the years, not only by observation but from working with him. When I think of what I have learned from him, the words Pursuit and Perseverance come to mind. Pursuit in regards to missions and Perseverance meaning to keep going and never give up.

MIKE HAS always had a heart for missions, and God has granted him success in all his missions endeavors. I learned from him the importance of giving to missions abroad and at home. I admire his heart for people and how he takes the Great Commission seriously to make sure others have the chance to hear about Jesus at all costs. I learned from him that you can't put a price tag on souls.

> I've had the honor to help host many missions banquets for Speed the Light alongside Mike while he served as the district youth director.

I've had the honor to help host many missions banquets for Speed the Light alongside Mike while he served as the district youth director. He does things with excellence, and it was always a privilege for me to be involved in anything he was doing. Missions is an important part of the church I pastor today, and part of the reason is because I took Mike's lessons to heart.

His pursuit to get the gospel message to the lost is heartfelt and a real concern to him. It should be our top priority as devoted Christ followers as well. Something that is missing in many churches today is compassion for lost people. It is something I don't feel can really be taught, it must be caught. It is caught from hanging around mission-minded people, and that is the kind of person Mike is.

> *He said to them, "Go into all the world and preach the gospel to all creation."*
>
> *Mark 16:15*

We have all been given the same commission: Go, disciple, baptize and teach. The way we fulfill it may be different, but the result is the same. Get people to Jesus and help them grow in their faith and become His disciple.

I have learned that for evangelism and missions to be caught, it requires being filled with the Holy Spirit. The infilling of the Spirit starts the fire and keeps it burning.

> *"But you will receive power when the Holy Spirit comes upon you. And you will be my witnesses, telling people about me everywhere—in Jerusalem, throughout Judea, in Samaria, and to the ends of the earth."*
>
> *Acts 1:8*

I often say that more than anything, I want to know Jesus and make Him known; and I want to make heaven my home and take as many people along with me as I can. That is only going to happen if I stay filled with the Holy Spirit who empowers us for this work and gives us the boldness to step out and do it. I remind myself that it is His work and that I can't save anyone. Only Jesus saves, and I am just a vessel He can use.

> After Jesus' resurrection, when they were filled with the Holy Spirit in the upper room, everything changed.

I am reminded of the difference the Holy Spirit makes when I think of Jesus' disciples. Before His crucifixion and death, they were timid, did not want to be associated with Him, denied knowing Him and ran when He was arrested, beaten and put on trial. After Jesus' resurrection, when they were filled with the Holy Spirit in the upper room, everything changed. They were no longer ashamed or afraid that they might be killed for their faith, and they spoke with certainty and boldness proclaiming Christ's resurrection. The Holy Spirit made the difference in their lives and still does for us today. We need the Holy Spirit.

After this prayer, the meeting place shook, and they were all filled with the Holy Spirit. Then they preached the word of God with boldness.

Acts 4:31

Only the Holy Spirit can enable us to stay on mission. The devil works hard and places all kinds of obstacles in our path to distract us and lead us off mission.

THE ENEMY wants nothing more than to stop the fire in us from starting, and if it has started, he takes extreme measures to put it out. Mike is a man filled with the Holy Spirit, one that the devil has fought hard but unsuccessfully to stop. Mike has his own journey from failure to faith. He tells in his book about the devil trying to take him down. Mike "caught" the heart of God to evangelize his community and the world, and the devil did not like it. The Holy Spirit is the reason why Mike is still standing.

> *Stay alert! Watch out for your great enemy, the devil. He prowls around like a roaring lion, looking for someone to devour.*
>
> 1 Peter 5:8

If the devil can devour us, he can stop our pursuit of God and the Great Commission from becoming reality in our lives. When you let this truth from the Word settle in your heart, you will recognize that the devil will attack us relentlessly. Even so, we can find rest and confidence in the fact that Jesus has already overcome the enemy. We can stand on God's promises while in the middle of battle and turmoil, and the enemy cannot touch us.

> *We are pressed on every side by troubles, but we are not crushed. We are perplexed, but not driven to despair. We are hunted down, but never abandoned by God. We get knocked*

down, but we are not destroyed. Through suffering, our bodies continue to share in the death of Jesus so that the life of Jesus may also be seen in our bodies.

2 Corinthians 4:8-10

Many times in my life and in my ministry I have battled feelings of despair. It can feel like I am being hunted and knocked down. Each time, I could reach out to Mike, and he would take time to remind me to get up and not give up, that I was not crushed or abandoned, and that God wasn't going to let the enemy destroy me. We all need a friend or spiritual father like that who will speak truth and reason into us until we can heal and think clearly.

I recall one of the darkest seasons of my life when it seemed like my world was crushing in all around me. I called Mike and told him I was done, that I was going to resign from the church and I needed a job. I still wanted to work for the Lord, I just did not want to be a lead pastor anymore. The pressure, scrutiny and pain that I was enduring was too much, and I wanted out. He told me he did not have a job for me, but he would find one and to come to his office and talk with him. That afternoon I spent the next six hours with him pouring out my heart and hurts as he listened and validated my pain. I believe he preached to me his entire book, *Never Give Up!*, because he knew I was about to. I am so thankful he was there for me.

Sometimes you just need someone to listen and feel your pain with you. Mike prayed for me and told me that he would help me find a job or hire me himself, but that I needed to take a month's sabbatical, to take a break from the ministry and rest. He told me to come back in a month and we would talk about it again. If I still felt the same way in a month, he would find me a job. He prayed a Holy Spirit-filled prayer over me that evening, and I left looking forward to resting and walking away from my position as lead pastor in only one more month.

> Mike checked on me periodically throughout the month, and nothing in my attitude changed for the first three weeks.

I asked my advisory council board from the church for the time off, and they graciously agreed. Mike checked on me periodically throughout the month, and nothing in my attitude changed for the first three weeks. In the third week, the enemy reared his head, and I came back a week early. I did not preach that week but was at the service. Things felt different, and my desperation to bail out as lead pastor wasn't so overwhelming.

I preached for the first time again the next Sunday. Mike called and asked me how it felt, and I said it actually felt pretty good. He said, "I knew it would," and that he knew I just needed to rest and walk away from it in order to miss it. He knew how the calling works and also how the devil works. Mike is a very smart man who is led by the Holy Spirit, and he spoke life into me as God used him to guide me through that dark time. I am forever grateful that God placed him in my life to speak truth and love me through my hurt.

MIKE HAS had his share of pain also and shared about it in his book, *Never Give Up! – Lessons the Lord Taught Me When I Wanted to Quit!* Isn't it amazing how God uses the things we go through to help others when they are going through something similar? I am thankful that God placed Mike in my life and the Holy Spirit led me to reach out to him when I needed to hear what he had to say at just the right time.

Life gets tough, ministry is tough, but we can't give up. Mike reminded me that *"any pastor worth his salt has gone through hell."* It is part of the fight, how the journey is navigated and the travail of running the race. We are on a journey, and we are heading to our destiny. Paul likens it to a race.

> **I press on to reach the end of the race and receive the heavenly prize for which God, through Christ Jesus, is calling us.**
>
> *Philippians 3:14*

Paul uses the analogy of a runner who focuses on the finish line ahead of him. This prevents distractions and keeps the runner from stumbling. In the spiritual sense he has a clear goal of reaching heaven and being with the Lord. He looks forward to the ultimate reward for his service. We must never forget what we are in pursuit of and persevere in the race that we are running so that we might reach the prize, which is to be with Christ eternally.

Paul is teaching us not to focus on the past, but to focus on what we can do today to live for Christ until we are one day with Him forever. We should live in such a way that we are always prepared, as we do not know just how close the finish line is. Whether we die or are taken in the rapture, we must persevere, stay in the race and run it faithfully.

> The truth is that when we surrender our lives to the Lord, the race and the battle just begins. The devil attacks those who desire to live righteous lives, not those who do not.

LIFE HAPPENS. I think many people, even Christians, think that when they give their lives to Christ, life from that moment will just be grand. Then the devil distracts us, for his goal is to take us out of the race and keep us from the prize that God has promised. The truth is that when we surrender our lives to the Lord, the race and the battle just begin. The devil attacks those who desire to live righteous lives, not those who do not. We actually become a target of the enemy when we commit our lives completely to Christ.

> **Many are the afflictions of the righteous, But the Lord delivers him out of them all. He guards all his bones; Not one of them is broken. Evil shall slay the wicked, and those who hate the righteous shall be condemned.**
>
> *Psalm 34:19-21 (ESV)*

The Hebrew word translated "deliver" in this verse also means "snatches away" and "rescues." The Lord will rescue the righteous person from times of affliction and evil people. This does not mean that we will not go through such times and not have to deal with evil people, but there is a way of rescue for the true believer.

David was hiding in a cave when he wrote this psalm. Even though he was in exile, he knew that the Lord would protect him from harm and deliver him eventually. This reminds us that being righteous doesn't guarantee that we will avoid affliction and evil. In fact, the passage says "many" are the afflictions of the righteous. It is only because we are in God's race and we are His children that He will deliver us and rescue us from tribulations and hard times. Jesus overcame the devil through His sacrifice on the cross. Attacks will come, but He has overcome the enemy, and all we need to do is stay faithful, run the race and cling to the promises of God's Word until we reach the finish line.

> **Blessed is the one who perseveres under trial because, having stood the test, that person will receive the crown of life that the Lord has promised to those who love him.**
>
> *James 1:12 (NIV)*

We often hear people refer to long-time saints in the church as having many jewels in their crowns in heaven. We really mean they have endured many trials in this life and have overcome through the power of faith. Let's not wish away our tribulations. God sees our tough times as an opportunity to develop our character to become more like Christ.

I know that Mike will have many jewels in his crown,

because God has developed his character repeatedly. That encourages me to be strong in my tough times, and I hope that one day I will also find many jewels in my heavenly crown. Until then, we must run the race God has set before us with diligence. We must stay in pursuit of the mission and make God known to those we meet on our journey. I encourage you to get in the race and take the Great Commission seriously. Run the race to win as many people as you can to Jesus while you can. I believe time is short and Jesus is coming sooner rather than later.

And now, dear children, continue in him, so that when he appears we may be confident and unashamed before him at his coming.

1 John 2:28 (NIV)

Mike has been and is a great example of pursuit and perseverance in my life and in the lives of all who know him. His love for the Lord, His work and His church is authentic, and he is committed to the race. Mike will win the prize, and when he does, his finish line will be filled with people whose lives have been touched by his love and ministry. If I get there first, I will be one of those, and if he gets there before me, I know I will be greeted with a smile from him, and he will say, "I told you to never give up. Just look at this!"

Dear friends, don't be surprised at the fiery trials you are going through, as if something strange were happening to you. Instead, be very glad—for these trials make you partners with Christ in his suffering, so that you will

have the wonderful joy of seeing his glory when it is revealed to all the world.

1 Peter 4:12-13

I want to close this chapter with a quote from Mike's book, *Never Give Up!,* that spoke to me personally.

> **I know you want to run. You want to pack it all up and head out the door. You want to check out and never come back. Not yet. Don't leave. Stay connected. It's during this time you will find the real you. It's the metal of character that's going to get you through the fire. The divorce, the failure, the moral collapse, the financial meltdown, or whatever it is that's propelling you to quit is only going to make you stronger.**
>
> – Mike Allard

Sometimes all you need are the faithful words of a friend to stay in the race.

Chapter 12

Messy & Miraculous

Bob Pesnell

I SHARED with you in the first chapter of this book that there was a deep secret my mother had kept. On January 18, 2021, I received shocking news that the father I thought was my dad for the last 53 years was not.

Bob Pesnell was my biological father.

This is the chapter designated to talk about him, but how do you write about someone you never met? So, I will share the messy story and share how God taught me through this revelation and did several miraculous things. I will share just how good God is and how His timing is always perfect.

God has a way of turning our messes into miracles and working things out for our good when we give it all to Him.

My discovery about my dad is noteworthy. I had been told in the past that I was partially German, Polish and a mix of something else from Louisiana. I did not know what that meant, so I wanted to find out. I had mentioned to my wife that I wanted to know more about my background and my origins. On Christmas, 2019, she gifted me an Ancestry DNA kit.

> I also noticed on my DNA results that there were no names or connection to my father's side of the family.

I took the test in the fall of 2020. In November, I received my results and found that I had no German in me. I was shocked to say the least, as I remember my grandmother Polnick spoke fluent German around me. I joked that I had learned how to cuss in German before I knew how to cuss in English. I also noticed on my DNA results that there were no names or connection to my father's side of the family, only a few from my mother's side and a bunch of others that appeared to be closely related but were unknown to me.

I pressed my mom for answers, and she quickly cut me off, claiming that the test had to be wrong. She had also done a DNA test and some of the things on her results "did not look correct" either.

Something was not right, so I shared my finding with my sister and asked for help. I had her take a DNA test, and we awaited her results. It came back that we were relatives and possibly cousins. The German roots and my dad's family names showed up on her results, I knew then that Rubin was not my biological father and wanted to know who was.

I reached out through the Ancestry website's email to

those on my profile that I was more closely related to and connected with a cousin and her daughter to begin my search. They were wonderful, kind and sincere to want to help me figure out how we were related. We spoke for several days and could not figure it out. I felt compelled to meet with my mom again and press her with the news that my sister and I were only half siblings. I reminded her before comforting her that DNA does not lie and that many people are even convicted and put on death row because of DNA results. I guess I thought that might scare her a little. She finally opened up and asked me if the last name Cannon was on my profile.

> My phone's text messages starting pinging, and my cousin told me that I was her uncle Bobby's son.

It wasn't, and I texted my cousins. They said no. Next my mom asked about the name Pesnell and whether it had come up on my DNA profile results.

It hadn't, and I texted my cousins once more. Within minutes my phone's text messages starting pinging, and my cousin told me that I was her uncle Bobby's son. I revealed to my mom that someone named Pesnell was my dad and asked her who he was.

Bob Pesnell owned the cleaners she worked for. I later found out that she was 20 years old, and he was 44 at the time. My mom and my dad had separated, and she was with Bob only that one time.

I told her that one time is all it takes.

MY MOM and I cried that day, and she apologized for keeping the secret from me that Rubin might not be my dad. In my mom's defense, there was a slim possibility that I could have been Rubin's son. They reunited and stayed married for several more years. She shared that when she told my dad, Rubin, that she was pregnant, he immediately denied that it was his. The truth is, no one knew whose I was, not even my mom. She told me long ago that I was named after her one true love, James. I learned after Mom's passing that James' last name was Cannon, and I assume that since she gave me the name Cannon first when trying to help me find out who my biological dad might be, that she always thought it was most likely him.

> The years of rejection I felt as a child from family, the partiality I had seen shown toward my sister and myself from each of my parents, began to make sense.

She was in complete shock to find out it was Mr. Pesnell. As for me? On that day something happened in me, and a light went off. The years of rejection I felt as a child from family, the partiality I had seen shown toward my sister and myself from each of my parents, began to make sense. The feelings I had carried for years were validated. I no longer felt crazy for my feelings of instability, distrust and even abandonment. I was free to heal.

MY MOM from as early and I could remember would not

let others correct me. Not even my dad. I now knew why. She never trusted his love for me or anyone else's love for that matter. This is probably the reason why I ended up being such a feminine guy, as I lacked correction and influence from a male figure in my life from an early age.

> I know she thought she was protecting me and did what she did out of love, but in reality, it caused me a lot of hurt.

My dad favored my sister, and because of that my mom favored me. Please know, I am not saying I did not feel loved by my dad, but he treated me differently and there was an obvious disconnect. My sister grew up with the same disconnect from my mom as she was partial to me in an effort to overcompensate for the love she felt I was missing from my father. I know she thought she was protecting me and did what she did out of love, but in reality, it caused me a lot of hurt and baggage I have had to work through.

This father disconnect was obvious, and once they divorced, it became greater. My dad was there, but he was absent, partly since we had a disconnect and partly because he remarried several times. With each marriage and divorce, we became less engaged in one another's lives and more distant. I loved him dearly, and as I said in an earlier chapter, he was an honest man and a man of honor, and he instilled the importance of both these things in my life without really even knowing it. I am blessed to have had Rubin as my dad, and I love and cherish his memory.

It was not until this came to light that I was able to understand the depth of all God had done in my life. The validation, clarification and understanding that this revelation brought me has helped me to process the magnitude of God's love for me and realize how in spite of the pain in my childhood that He had a plan and was working in my life.

THERE WERE many more messy things about my childhood, and I shared some of those in the beginning of this book. I chose not to focus on the negative and dwell on the messy but to celebrate the miraculous things that came out of the messy.

> Six months after the revelation about my biological father, my mother went to be with the Lord.

Six months after the revelation about my biological father, my mother went to be with the Lord. She was a strong woman and lived much of her life knowing the Lord but not living for Him. The last two years of her life, I watched the Holy Spirit work in her in a mighty way. I had been her son for 52 years, but I had the honor of becoming her pastor. As I am writing this, the one-year anniversary of her death is approaching quickly, and I am filled with different emotions but grateful that she came to know the Lord personally and completely put her trust in Him. Something changed in her after the revelation about my dad. I realize now that a great weight had been lifted off her just before her death. The secret she had kept, the question of who my biological father was, had been cleared, and she was free from things that had been tucked away in darkness.

My sister Tammie even received healing in all of this, as she had carried around years of hurt because my mom had favored me and seemed to resent her because of the situation. Before my mom's passing, I was able to discuss these feelings about how Tammie felt, and God provided a special opportunity for her and my sister to talk that brought healing to them.

> Hurt people hurt people, and my mom carried around a lot of hurt from her childhood.

Hurt people hurt people, and my mom carried around a lot of hurt from her childhood and upbringing that brought about many insecurities and bad decisions. I thank God that she found the grace of God, and I am glad I did also. God was so gracious to allow this weight to be lifted in her life, my sister's life and my life just months before Mom's passing. That alone is miraculous.

I WAS heartbroken at the loss of my mom, but I also had hope. I could rejoice in the freedom she received and that my prayers had been answered. All I ever wanted was to know that she would be in heaven with me one day, and I celebrate that she made it. I joked at her funeral that she was "a tough one," and she was, but she surrendered her life to the Lord in a beautiful and miraculous way, and I know today that she is not just healed but whole standing in the presence of the King of Kings and Lord of Lords.

Another miracle that happened from the discovery of Bob Pesnell as my biological father is that I have additional family. I have three new half siblings and nieces and nephews. It has been such a joy to connect with my older sister Gerri at this time in my life. I needed her. God knew the void I would be facing when my mom left for heaven and brought Gerri into my life at just the right time. Gerri needed me, too, and both of us felt an immediate and special bond. We are brother and sister in the Lord and in heart.

God knew the void I would be facing when my mom left for heaven and brought Gerri into my life at just the right time.

Gerri and I are creating memories, and our love for the Lord is our common ground. Both her parents and her close relatives have passed away, and life gets lonely for her at times. During the pandemic, she isolated and hardly left her house except for church. She said when I came into her life that things changed. She said she told a friend, *"All my life God knew this day would come and it would change my life."* Our meeting changed both of our lives! We also found out that we had lived in the same area of town for years and attended some of the same concerts. God was gracious to us both when He allowed us to find one another.

Gerri and I have both looked at our church friends like our family and both have a love for the church choir. I was a choir director, and she has been an alto in the choir for over forty years. So much in common for two people who had never met.

> You had no idea that you needed another sibling, but with him [James], you won the lottery!

Gerri's friend Sandy told her, *"James is living proof of God's immeasurable riches and perfect timing. You were in your sixties when God dropped a baby brother into your life. You had no idea that you needed another sibling, but with him, you won the lottery! Suddenly you have a brother with a heart who loves his God, his family and his church – and cares about you! How cool is that? James is also a good example of God's sense of humor and love. Zephaniah 3:17 tells us He 'will rejoice over you with singing.' Don't you just know that in earlier days, months and years, God chuckled to Himself and said, 'Just hold on, Gerri ... just you wait until you see what I'm bringing into your life!' Anytime you feel discouraged and wonder what God is doing in your life, you need to take a minute, think about James and give God thanks!"*

I am humbled by what Sandy said, but I feel the blessing is mine in learning about and finding Gerri. Before my mom passed, she and Gerri got to meet, and together we were all able to enjoy Mother's Day and Father's Day in the final year of my mom's life. Those are memories I will forever cherish. God's timing in all of this is nothing short of miraculous. God has everything all figured out.

There is a time for everything, and a season for every activity under the heavens:

Ecclesiastes 3:1 (NIV)

At the right time, God will provide our needs. At the right time, God will deliver us. At the right time, God will rescue you and me. As a loving Father, at the right time He will provide what we need and fill any void that we lack.

I learned a little about my biological dad
from my sister Gerri.

I never got to meet Bob Pesnell, He passed away on May 25, 1995. I learned a little about my biological dad from my sister Gerri. He was a great painter, businessman and leader in his community. He had a big heart and was always willing to help those in need. I was recently at a ball game with her and my family. I saw some friends who had four small children and went over to say hello. Their children started saying, "I'm hungry." So, I asked what they wanted to eat and was able to fulfill their requests. Gerri told my wife, "That's something that Dad would do." He was a giver and had a big heart for all people and especially children.

When I saw Bob's picture for the first time, I realized where my 18-year-old son Jayden got his curly dark hair. The mystery of his curls was solved. I would have loved to have gotten to know Bob, but that didn't happen this side of heaven. My hope is that one day we will all be in heaven together.

I recently had the opportunity to meet my other sister Tonya and begin a relationship with her. We have our creative side in common and we were shocked after talking that she was employed at the hospital where my mom went and did charity work. When I showed her my mom's photograph she said, "I know her." Such a small world. I look forward to getting to know her better and making memories with her.

MY LIFE has taken many turns and many twists. I have questioned why I have had to deal with the pain and hurt I have endured. If I am being honest, I have never gotten an answer from Him, but one thing I do know is that from dealing with it, I was forced to draw closer to Him. Because of it, I know Him better, and I would not trade that closeness for anything.

> ***I consider that our present sufferings are not worth comparing with the glory that will be revealed in us.***
>
> *Romans 8:18 (NIV)*

Nothing in life gets wasted for a child of God. He will use it for His glory and reveal Himself in a real way. God has a history of turning our messes into miracles and turning things around.

I can't help but be reminded that the earthly line from which Jesus was born was messy. Jesus came from a long line of outsiders, outlaws, scoundrels and sinners. We can't escape the reality that the lives of each of the women chosen to be included in His lineage were touched by sexual scandal. Tamar was a prostitute; Rahab ran a brothel; and Ruth the Moabite was part of the lineage of Lot.

Do you remember Lot? He was the guy who impregnated his daughters while drunk.

Jesus comes from the line of David who committed adultery and murder. Bathsheba was used sexually by David which led to an unexpected pregnancy. But she, too, through her son Solomon, found her way into the family of Jesus. All the sexual scandal in the lives of these women prepares us for the great scandal to come: the pregnancy of unwed Mary, the mother of Jesus. It was His Father in heaven's bloodline that made Him our Savior. I am thankful that God uses messy people to accomplish miraculous things when they repent and surrender to Him. I certainly would not be pastoring a church if that were not the case.

> **God chose things despised by the world, things counted as nothing at all, and used them to bring to nothing what the world considers important.**
>
> 1 Corinthians 1:28

I am grateful that God saved me and that I responded to His voice to surrender my life to Him. It was the greatest decision I have ever made. When He took over, things changed. I stand amazed at how God has chosen to use me in the way that He has. Imperfect people who surrender to a perfect God produce miraculous results. I am humbled and honored by His grace.

We all had a past before Jesus came into our lives and

took our sin away. He is a good and gracious God who loves us unconditionally in spite of our shortcomings and faults. There will be no perfect people in heaven, only forgiven people. I want to remind you that it does not matter where you came from, it matters where you are going. There is no mess too big that God cannot miraculously turn it around.

Jesus looked at them and said, "With man this is impossible, but not with God; all things are possible with God."

Mark 10:27 (NIV)

God the Father in every season strategically placed men (and even women) along the path of this fatherless boy's life in order to teach me about Him and reveal His truth. These men impacted my life as I saw the good things and God things operating in my interaction with each of them. From their examples, as the work of the Holy Spirit in my life worked through the pain, I learned to be the man of God, husband, father, son, brother, friend and pastor that I am. God is good!

I can't help but close this chapter by referencing a song of praise that is dear to my heart. It's *Goodness of God* from Bethel music. My youngest daughter, Brighten, sang it at my mom's funeral. It has become my anthem in this season of my life. It talks about the goodness of God and how His mercy never fails us from the time we arise each morning until we go to bed at night.

The song ends with claiming God as a father and a friend and rejoicing that we have lived in His goodness. Wow! That will make you want to sing and rejoice in Him!

Chapter 13

My Two Greatest Teachers

The Holy Spirit & Pain

I TRULY have been blessed to have all the men in my life that God has placed in my path to show me His heart and set an example before me of what a Godly man, husband and father should look like. Just because you are born fatherless or your father was absent does not mean that you are meant to stay that way. As children of God, we have a Heavenly Father who desires more than anything to fill that void and teach us truth and what we need to know.

As I come to the close of this book with this final chapter, I want to share about the two greatest teachers God used to help me learn some of my toughest lessons and greatest truths in life – the Holy Spirit and Pain.

I have shared how God used other men and people throughout this book, but He Himself – God the Holy Spirit – has taught me the most. We are drawn to the saving knowledge of Christ through revelation from the work of the Holy Spirit. Once we repent, at salvation the Holy Spirit takes residence in us. This is the first baptism of salvation. The second baptism we do out of obedience to the scriptures, and we follow this up in water baptism and publicly profess Jesus as our Lord.

> This baptism can be confusing to some people, but it is found in all four of the gospels and in the book of Acts, and it is still for people today.

Water baptism represents that we have been cleansed from our sins, forgiven and have become a creation in Christ. Many Christians stop at this point and fail to experience the third powerful baptism that Jesus Himself promises to us. This baptism can be confusing to some people, but it is found in all four of the gospels and in the book of Acts, and it is still for people today.

It is the baptism of the infilling of the Holy Spirit.

The word baptism in the original Greek means the process of immersion, submersion and emergence. When you think of this third baptism, think of it as not just having the Holy Spirit in your life, but letting Him fill your life completely, in every area and every part of who you are. When we welcome this third baptism, we experience a Spirit-led life, and we find a faithful friend who is with us to help us, comfort us, teach us, remind us, convict us and impart special gifts on us to use for God's glory.

Simply put, at salvation we get the Holy Spirit, but when we are filled with the Holy Spirit, He gets all of us.

> *But when the Father sends the Advocate as my representative—that is, the Holy Spirit—he will teach you everything and will remind you of everything I have told you.*
>
> *John 14:26*

I am filled and baptized in and with God – the Holy Spirit. He is part of the Triune Godhead that we know and serve, and He is a person. I have found that the greatest way God is a Father to the fatherless is by the Holy Spirit. Although God placed father-like men in my life to set an example and for me to learn from, the Holy Spirit helped me sort through what I was learning and helped me make sense of it all by orchestrating my path and enabling me to find confirmation about what I was learning and by giving me a discerning spirit. Remember me saying at the beginning that none of the men I learned from were perfect, that they all had flaws? The Holy Spirit is not flawed, and when He gives revelation, it is always right and can be completely trusted. I am a little hardheaded, so sometimes to get through to me, He must give me multiple confirmations and tell me things more than once. I am thankful our God knows us and is patient with us.

The Holy Spirit has been my greatest source of revelation, wisdom and power. I never want to live a day without Him.

> *But it was to us that God revealed these things by his Spirit. For his Spirit searches out everything and shows us God's deep secrets. No one can know a person's thoughts except*

that person's own spirit, and no one can know God's thoughts except God's own Spirit. And we have received God's Spirit (not the world's spirit), so we can know the wonderful things God has freely given us.

1 Corinthians 2:10-12

The Holy Spirit has worked in my life for many years and has taught me and revealed the heart of God to me greater than anyone else. The Holy Spirit has taught me the truth in scripture. He gives me an understanding of what God is trying to say as I mediate on His Word. The Holy Spirit leads me to a timely Word that I need for whatever current situation or circumstance I find myself in.

The Holy Spirit corrects me and lets me know when I am wrong.

My Father – the Holy Spirit – helps me to discern what is truth and what is not. He goes before me and reveals things that I cannot see in the natural and gives me eyes to see what is happening in the spiritual. He allows me to see into the hurting hearts of others and be sensitive to love them through their own pain.

The Holy Spirit corrects me and lets me know when I am wrong. He convicts without condemnation and reminds me that God is faithful to forgive me if I will go to Him and confess my sin.

Best of all, the Holy Spirit tells me I am loved.

The Holy Spirit has helped me develop the character

of God in my life – the Fruit of His Spirit – which changes me and helps me become more like Jesus. He lays on my heart the things that are dear to the heart of God. The Holy Spirit keeps me in the know and points out the work God has for me to do. The Holy Spirit leads me to the right people to teach me and impact my life.

The Holy Spirit prepares me for things to come and reminds me that God is with me. He brings to my memory the Word of God in regard to what is happening and lets me know that the outcome will be used for my good.

> Our season of the Jezebel spirit had started. We returned home to face the pain of betrayal and had to face the Jezebel spirit head on.

Gina and I went to a pastors' conference, and we kept hearing the same message at the conference over and over. It had to do with the Jezebel spirit and how it operates in the church. It was a message of betrayal as well. While we listened, we wondered why we were hearing so much about this, because we did not feel it was for us at the season of life we were in. As we discussed it, I got a text that revealed why we were hearing repeatedly about the Jezebel spirit.

Our season of the Jezebel spirit had started. We returned home to face the pain of betrayal and had to face the Jezebel spirit head on. The Holy Spirit was preparing us to deal with what was coming. We realized this, and I was thankful for the warning. We also knew that because He had prepared us, He would be with us through it.

I have told you all this so that you may have peace in me. Here on earth you will have many trials and sorrows. But take heart, because I have overcome the world.

John 16:33

In a very sweet way, the Holy Spirit prepared me for my mom's death. He placed me in a situation, and He and I had an in-depth conversation where He let me know that a time was coming when I would need to say goodbye and let her go. I did a lot of begging for more time, but through several confirmations, I knew the time would be sooner than I thought and that it was time for her to go, even though it would be painful. I was heartbroken but I had hope.

The truth of our existence is that pain happens.

THE HOLY SPIRIT has always taught me and helped me work through my pain. Yes, **pain** has been a great teacher. The Holy Spirit with me in the middle of my pain is the best coach for getting the most out of the lessons God wants me to internalize.

The truth of our existence is that pain happens. Sometimes it is self-inflicted but mostly it is not. As children of God, we have a Father in heaven who will use our pain for good if we let Him. He will use all things good and bad for His purpose, and this includes pain.

When our youngest daughter, Brighten, was born, I was coming out of a dark season. Her arrival ushered in an even darker season as we learned she was born with birth defects. The multiple problems we faced sent me into a downward spiral. My wife was a champ, and when I think back to that time, it hurts me to think about how she must have hurt, too, but I was too focused on how Brighten's condition would affect me and "my" ministry. The Lord revealed that the ministry was not mine. It was His, and it was going to look like He wanted it to look.

> I had this idea that if I kept working hard for Him, He would make everything in my life perfect.

It was in that season that I stopped focusing on trying to please people all the time and to please God. I also learned to slow down and sit at the Lord's feet more. I had been so busy working for Him that things got out of balance, and I was neglecting time with Him. I had this idea that if I kept working hard for Him, He would make everything in my life perfect. I was dumb to think that, as scripture tells us that trials and tribulations will come, and God will be with us when they do. We will overcome them because He is our overcomer (John 16:33). It is in those seasons we come to know Him deeper.

Brighten has become a source God has used to brighten my days, and He used the pain of this circumstance to take me to another level. She is a gift, as all my kids are, but He blessed our family with someone extra special when He sent her to us. To this day, when life gets crazy, trials seem unbearable and the pain gets great, I walk away from it all and go find Brighten, because her presence makes things better. I learned family was more important in my pain.

IN PAIN I learned to forgive. I went through a lot growing up, and when I thought about all that happened to me and all I endured, I relived the pain.

> I began to pray for their healing and their salvation.

It was in those moments of thinking about those things that the Holy Spirit began to convict me of the bitterness and resentment I held, and that I must forgive those who inflicted the hurt and rejection in my life. I was able to see those people the way God saw them and understand that hurt people hurt people, and that they need Jesus too. I began to pray for their healing and their salvation.

Through a painful situation of rejection, I learned to listen and obey God's voice, not man's. If I had not learned this, I would have never stepped out in obedience and planted the church I now pastor. Good-hearted men can sometimes appear to offer you Godly wisdom, but they still fight the flesh's desire to benefit themselves. You must learn to hear the voice of God for yourself and not depend on someone else to tell you what they think God wants you to do. The Holy Spirit is good at helping you hear God's voice and not man's.

In pain I learned the heart of the Heavenly Father and how He would always be with me. God does not keep the pain away, rather, He uses it to teach us things. He never promised us that we won't go through trials and tribulations. He only promised us that we would not be alone.

> **This is my command—be strong and courageous! Do not be afraid or discouraged. For the LORD your God is with you wherever you go.**
>
> Joshua 1:9

Most people first understand their need for a Savior during painful and desperate situations and circumstances. Pain has a way of reminding us that we are not in charge in life, and the realization causes us to reach to the One who is in charge and make Jesus Christ the Lord of their lives. Pain makes us long for hope, and hope is found in Christ alone.

In pain, we have a greater revelation of Jesus. Our faith is put to the test in pain, but Jesus promises to restore us and make us stronger from our suffering.

God uses our pain to strengthen us and encourage others to trust Him and believe that He is working despite what we see.

> **And the God of all grace, who called you to his eternal glory in Christ, after you have suffered a little while, will himself restore you and make you strong, firm and steadfast. To him be the power for ever and ever. Amen.**
>
> 1 Peter 5:10-11 (NIV)

I have learned that pain is part of the process when you are a leader. You will be misunderstood, talked about, betrayed, rejected and hurt. All Jesus' disciples experienced this, and many suffered a martyr's death. It will not be any different for us as modern-day disciples. In times when I have had to go through pain and rejection as a leader, the Holy Spirit has reminded me of this passage:

He was despised and rejected by mankind, a man of suffering, and familiar with pain. Like one from whom people hide their faces he was despised, and we held him in low esteem.

Isaiah 53:3 (NIV)

The cost of following Jesus can be painful but will be worth it in the end. The Bible tells us to take up our cross and follow Jesus (Luke 9:23). Carrying a cross is not easy. It was painful for Jesus and at times will be painful for us. Jesus was praised one day and spat upon the next, and we should not expect anything less. In pain we grow. God does not let anything we go through be wasted.

Dear brothers and sisters, when troubles of any kind come your way, consider it an opportunity for great joy. For you know that when your faith is tested, your endurance has a chance to grow. So let it grow, for when your endurance is fully developed, you will be perfect and complete, needing nothing.

James 1:2-4

Pain is the threshold for spiritual growth. God uses it to help us grow. When you have spiritual growing pains, **God is paving the way for something new**. Perhaps for wisdom, perhaps for patience but always perseverance. We must trust Him and the process in order to grow.

God uses our pain. A great example of this is found in the story of Paul and Silas. In Philippi, Paul and Silas were beaten in public and taken to prison. Word began to spread throughout the region of the great pain they were suffering for sharing the message of Jesus. Imagine the excitement that took place as the news began to spread about the details of the midnight song, earthquake and jailer's conversion.

Days prior to their miraculous release, Paul and Silas must have been screaming their prayers to God and begging for help. The relief didn't come right away, but the message of Christ exploded in that city, in a large part because of the unfair suffering they'd known. The pain Paul and Silas went through served a greater purpose as God used it to spread the gospel message.

Like Paul and Silas, most of us can't see the purpose of our pain right at first, but it does not mean that God does not have one. God is always working, and the things He does are done with eternity in mind.

EVERY INDIVIDUAL God used in a mighty way throughout scripture went through times of pain and hardship. Moses had to flee his family who wanted to kill him; Elijah had people wanting him dead; Queen Esther risked her life in order to save the Jewish people; David had to hide in the mountains because King Saul wanted to kill him; and most of Jesus' disciples were killed for their commitment to Christ. Jesus Himself was beaten and crucified for us. If we want to be used mightily by God, we must get used to the pain. Pain is part of the process of complete surrender to God.

> Our pain and suffering often sets us up to see God's supernatural work in our lives.

Our pain and suffering often sets us up to see God's supernatural work in our lives. We learn how powerful He is and that He is still in the miracle-working business. I have witnessed this repeatedly as friends and acquaintances are healed from sickness or God intervenes in a situation in a miraculous way. When He does this in our pain, He gets all the glory, and we get the testimony to share.

This has happened countless times in my own life. As a teenager I was diagnosed with a tumor and went to a revival. I was prayed over, went back to the doctor and was told nothing was there. When our daughter Brighten was born, we were told that she might never walk or talk, and now she is on the go everywhere on two legs, never shuts up and sings to the Lord all the time. God intervened in my pain in several dark times of my life and got me the help I needed at just the right time. Financial breakthroughs happened at just the right time and from out of nowhere or from the least expected place.

It is painful while we are in the middle of trouble, but it is miraculous when God shows up in a powerful way and makes a way where there seems to be no way. What I'm saying is that our pain in this world is temporary. Pain and suffering will not last forever. We have the promise of this in the Word of God:

He will wipe every tear from their eyes, and there will be no more death or sorrow or crying or pain. All these things are gone forever.

Revelation 21:4

Jesus is coming. Our pain and suffering will not be totally forgotten, but the sting of it will be gone, and eternity will be even greater as a result with no pain, no tears, no turmoil and no hurts or heartaches.

Most of my pain in spiritual leadership has arisen from people in the church, what we might call "pastoring pain." God has taught me to accept that this is my world and what I do. People are not perfect, not even church people; and pain is something you will experience in life no matter where you are.

I have always learned through my pain. In one of my darkest pain-filled hours, a pastor friend gave me a book called *Leadership Pain – The Classroom for Growth* by Samuel Chand. It was a game changer for me, and I highly recommend it for all pastors to read. I think the greatest thing I got out of it was that I wasn't the only one hurting like I was with "pastoring pain."

The Holy Spirit and pain work together in the life of the believer to reveal and teach us many things. But for them to do that, we must be open and welcome the infilling work of the Holy Spirit in our lives and embrace the pain that comes with courage. This is one of the greatest ways the Heavenly Father teaches me fatherly lessons and directs my path according to His will.

Life is not painless; it is actually painful, but God can use even the pain. Paul encouraged the church at Corinth (and the church today) with these words:

> **Therefore we do not lose heart. Though outwardly we are wasting away, yet inwardly we are being renewed day by day. For our light and momentary troubles are achieving for us an eternal glory that far outweighs them all.**
>
> 2 Corinthians 4:16-17 (NIV)

I want to close this final chapter with a prayer of thanksgiving to the Lord for the Holy Spirit and how He has used my pain to teach me. I also want to thank Him for filling that father void and becoming my Heavenly Father. As you read this, I pray that you will make this your prayer also.

> *Heavenly Father, thank You for being the Father I need. I never knew love until I met You and found Your unconditional love. I thank You for the men that You placed in my life to teach me Your ways and how to be a husband, father and pastor. I am grateful for each one listed in this book and for many others that aren't.*
>
> *Thank You, Holy Spirit, for drawing me to a saving knowledge of who Jesus is and filling me with Your Spirit to live an overcoming life of power while living in the world full of heartache, hurt and tribulation. I am thankful that as a*

Heavenly Father You sent the Word that became flesh by sending Jesus Your only Son to redeem us. Holy Spirit, help me to always keep the Word daily as a lamp before my feet and a light for my path.

Thank You for every lesson I have learned through pain. Lord, I pray that every person that ever reads this book will know You as Father God and allow You to fill any void that is lacking in their lives. I also pray that You would open any hurting eyes to see those You have placed around them to fill the father void and teach them about You.

Cause each reader to make themselves available to those that You place in their paths that need mentoring, direction and to experience Your love and wisdom and know You more. In Jesus' name I pray, Amen.

www.ingramcontent.com/pod-product-compliance
Lightning Source LLC
Chambersburg PA
CBHW061637040426
42446CB00010B/1468